"Ocean in view! O! the joy."

William Clark November 7th 1805.
Clark was premature in his exuberance, for what he had actually seen was the Columbian estuary, not the ocean. Still, the moments when dreams seem real remain forever the joy of experience and help define the personal version of the journey. They are plentiful when you come find Washington.

Message from
The Publisher

This unique visual source book begins with an overview of Washington State. Hundreds of stunning photos invite you to explore the hidden treasures of the state.

The unique homes reflect the interests, travels and pursuits of the owners. Whether humble or grand, rural retreats, elegant townhouses or hi-tech yachts, these dream homes express the feelings about living in the state of Washington. Section by section the book is filled with over 500 full color photographs of homes that accommodate varying budgets and lifestyles.

So, sit back, draw upon some creative daydreaming and uncover a variety of visions of your ideal home.

Ron Wilks, Publisher
RhinoBooks, LLC

"The mountains are high with lush forests and pristine alpine lakes hidden from the too casual viewer. Walk in the quiet of these ancient forests and peer into the glass of the alpine lakes."

Washington Office Of Tourism

Photo left: Charles Gurche. Photo right: Rob Perry & Charles Gurche

Washington

Area: 63,192 square miles, 1,483 miles of inland water surface
Population (2000): 5,894,121, 21% increase since 1990 census
Capitol and largest city: Olympia, Seattle
Statehood: November 11, 1889
Highest point: Mt. Rainier 14,410 ft
Lowest point: Sea Level
Nickname: Evergreen State
Motto: Alki (By and By)
State bird: Willow Goldfinch
State flower: Western Rhododendron
State tree: Western Hemlock

- The state of Washington is the only state to be named after a United States president.

- Washington produces more apples than any other state in the union. According to the Guinness Book of World Records, the largest apple pie ever made was in Wenatchee, weighing in at 15 tons!

- Washington's wine appellations boast over 28,000 acres, making it second only to California in U.S. grapevine acreage.

- Washington has more glaciers than the other 47 contiguous states combined. 80% of the glacial ice in the U.S is found in Washington State.

- There are over 40,000 miles of rivers and streams and more than 8,000 lakes in the state..

- Snoqualmie Falls are 100 feet higher than Niagara Falls.

- Washington has 3 National Parks, 9 National Forests and 100 State Parks.

- The Olympic National Park is home to about 5,000 Roosevelt Elk, the largest number of the species anywhere.

- The Ginkgo Petrified Forest is the largest in the world.

- Southeastern Washington is home to Hells Canyon, the deepest river gorge in North America. It averages 5,500 feet in depth over a 40-mile section of its 100-mile length.

- Mt. Rainier is an active volcano encased in more than 35 square miles of snow and ice. It is visited by almost 1.5 million tourists each year.

- Spokane was the smallest city in size to host a World's Fair - 1974.

- Everett is the site of the world's largest building, Boeing's final assembly plant

- La Push is the western most town in the contiguous United States.

- Washington is the birthplace of both Jimi Hendrix (Seattle) and Bing Crosby (Tacoma).

- Washington is the home of the United States wealthiest man, Microsoft's Bill Gates.

- Starbucks, the biggest coffee chain in the world, was founded in Seattle.

- Kennewick Man, found in 1996 along the shores of Columbia Park in Kennewick, is one of the oldest and most complete skeletons ever found in the America's. He is estimated to be nearly 9,000 years old!

- Bigfoot, also known as Sasquatch, gained official status in 1975. That year the Army Corps of Engineers published an environmental atlas that first recognized Sasquatch as a species indigenous to Washington State.

- Highest temperature recorded: 118 degrees - August 5th, 1961 at Ice Harbor Dam.

- Lowest temperature recorded: -48 degrees - December 30th, 1968 at Mazama and Winthrop.

- At low tide, there can be up to 786 islands in the Puget Sound.

Comb the beach, fish the rivers, delve deep into the forest, ride bikes on rolling roads, watch for whales, hike to a summit and join the eagles, walk in the quiet of ancient forests, swim in seas of wildflowers, surf and snowboard in the same day, raft through the deepest canyon, search for the last herd of wild caribou, climb on the back of a volcano, windsurf with the world's best.

A land of majestic forests, snow-clad mountains, sparkling blue waters, vast and semi-desert lands and rolling green hills, Washington State is a wonderful place. But most of all, when you come to Washington, come to meet the people.

Photo Left: Charles Gurche, Top: Steve Keating, and Michael Mathers

Washington State's quality of life is exceptional. Continually rated as one of the most livable states in the nation, the diverse climate and terrain offer a myriad of outdoor activities. Ski down world-class slopes, scale 14,411 foot Mt. Rainier, windsurf on the Columbia Gorge, backpack through emerald stands of pristine forests, travel to the Eastern desert where 10,000 years ago the first Native Americans roamed, or follow the Lewis and Clark trail as they passed through in 1805.

Come Find Washington

discover

Once it took "courage undaunted" to cross the state. Today, the only requirement is a willingness to uncover the diversity that makes Washington such a great place to live.

Top: Comet Falls, Mt. Rainier National Park. Photo: Rob Perry

Top right: Parasailing the San Juan Islands. Photo: Chris Amonson

Bottom left: Wild flowers in Okanogan County. Photo: Charles Gurche

Bottom right: Winter view, WA Photo: Snowdragon Adventure shots

freedom, challenge, renewal . . . the land lights a fire within us

WASHINGTON
Mountains

"Of all the fire mountains, which like beacons, once blazed along the Pacific Coast, Mount Rainier is the noblest."

--John Muir

Photo opposite page: Mt. Rainier. At 14,411 feet, "The Mountain" is one of the snowiest places on the planet. Walk or hike the countless trails and spy on glaciers while standing amidst a sea of wildflowers. Even a short hike trades the crowds in for a wilderness of huge, ancient trees, alpine glades, icy-cold tumbling streams and ancient glaciers. Photo: Charles Gurche

Photo top: Mt. Adams. One of the largest volcanoes in the Cascade Range, Mt. Adams towers 12,276 feet above sea level. In the summer, wildflowers blanket much of the mountain in a surreal array of color. Reached most rapidly from Trout Lake, endless miles of trails await explorers on foot or horseback. Photo: Peter Nelson

Photo center: Mt. Baker rises 10,778 feet above sea level in the center of the Mt. Baker Wilderness. Though perpetually covered in snow and ice, it is the second most active volcano in the Cascade Range. In 1999, Mt. Baker set the new world's record for the most snowfall ever measured in a single season-- 1,140 inches (95 feet). Photo: Charles Gurche

Photo bottom: Mount St. Helens. On May 18, 1980, the country's only active volcano woke with the force of a hydrogen bomb. Scientists have called the Mount St. Helens' eruption the greatest natural disaster in United States history. Today you can witness firsthand the land being reborn. Some plant life and animals have returned and a new dome is forming. Photo: Martin Bydalek

Mount St. Helens view from Yale Lake, Washington

The pristine beauty of Mount St. Helens and the surrounding countryside were forever changed at 8:32 Sunday morning, May 18, 1980 when the mountain erupted and the north face collapsed. At the same time a mushroom-shaped column of ash rose thousands of feet skyward and drifted downwind, turning day into night as dark, gray ash fell over eastern Washington and beyond. The eruption lasted 9 hours, but Mount St. Helens and the surrounding landscape were dramatically changed within moments.

Photos by: Steve Terrill

WASHINGTON
Geography

On November 11, 1889, Washington became the 42nd State to enter the Union. It is nicknamed "The Evergreen State" for its abundant evergreen forests.

"I think that what happens when places are invented is something like this: We are the creators, the inventors of the places around us. We invest certain parts of the earth as special, set aside and set apart from other parts. Often we name those places, drawing on experience or desire or personal ambition. Thus, we have Cape Disappointment, Cape Flattery, Deception Pass, Bellevue, Longview, Richland, Sunnyside, Vancouver, Mt. Adams, and Puget Sound. We do that naming and setting apart on a large scale and we call those things "regions". We do it on a small, perhaps more intimate scale, and we use the word "place". Lewis and Clark did both throughout their journey into the West. They invented places and fashioned regions." James Ronda, COLUMBIA Magazine - Spring 2002

Washington's landscape has over 40,000 miles of rivers and streams, dotted by nearly 8,000 lakes and framed by 520 miles of pacific coastline. Much of Washington's natural wonders of mountains, forests, lakes and shorelines are preserved within the state's three national parks, nine national forests and over one hundred state parks, recreation areas, and wildlife preserves.

In Washington you will find majestic forests, snow-clad mountains, the mighty Pacific Ocean and the sparkling blue inland waters of Puget Sound, as well as the vast and semi-desert lands of the interior and, further east, the rolling green hills of the Palouse. Mt. Baker and Mt. Rainer stand out above the rest of the Cascade Range and divide the state into two very different halves. Most of the state has a mild climate without the extremes experienced in many other parts of the USA. Many ski slopes are just an hour away from the main cities; some are in isolated resort areas. The natural beauty of the state is never too far to seek. Golf, sailing, scuba-diving, hiking, camping, are all popular activities, while the Columbia Gorge is renowned for wind-surfing.

State of Washington "The Evergreen State"

Opposite page: Columbia River
Photo: Charles Gurche

Regions

Western   page 18
Central   page 39
Eastern   page 52

Washington

The Islands

This legendary archipelago was a gift of the glaciers that covered Washington 15 thousand years ago. Whether you live here or are visiting, prepare to set your watch for "Island Time."

Whidbey Island: Whidbey Island is the largest of five islands that make up Island County. You can reach the island by driving over the majestic Deception Pass Bridge at the northern tip of the island. Whidbey Island is known for its quaint inns, historic towns, white oak forests and Ebey's Landing National Historic Reserve - 17,000 acres of protected nature and historic sites.

Photo: Steve Terrill, Deception Pass

Camano Island State Park is a popular escape that encompasses 134 acres of protected forest and more than a mile of coastline.

Bainbridge Island: Bainbridge Island is one of the largest islands in Puget Sound. In 1991 the people of Bainbridge Island voted to make their entire island the city of Bainbridge Island. Island attractions include the village of Winslow that offers waterfront strolls, quaint shops, and several fine cafes and restaurants. The 150 acre Bloedel Reserve is a country estate of manicured lawns, forests and ponds. Visitors can enjoy a winery tour at the Bainbridge Island Winery, shopping at the local Farmer's Market, a movie at the theatre or learn some history at the Bainbridge Island Historical Museum. The Island is also home to numerous art galleries, boutiques and antique shops.

San Juan Island: The Island is located approximately 90 miles north of Seattle and 80 miles south of Vancouver, British Columbia. While visiting San Juan Island, be sure to spend time enjoying the parks and historic port locations of both Friday Harbor and Roche Harbor Village where you will go back in time with the Victorian Gardens and historical buildings. The topography of San Juan Island ranges from mountainous on the north end to farmland in the central valleys and south end.

The San Juan Islands lie in the rain shadow of the Olympic Peninsula and enjoy some of the best weather in the Pacific Northwest. Created during the Ice Age, the San Juans were recently named the #2 island destination in the Continental U.S. and Canada. Part of the charm of the San Juans is that each island seems to have a character of its own, both in terms of geography and of the lifestyle of the people who live there. There are many days when it will be raining in Seattle or Vancouver, but clear and sunny on the islands.

Blakely Island: Blakely Island is unique among Washington State's San Juan Islands. This 4,700-acre island is the largest of the non-ferry served islands in San Juan County. Two 70-acre, spring fed freshwater lakes are protected by 3000 acres of forestland. They offer exceptional fishing, swimming and boating. If privacy is what you are looking for, you could find yourself completely alone in nature here.

Camano Island: Camano Island is just a 1-hour drive from either Seattle or the Canadian border. Many visitors find that Camano is the perfect "base camp" from which to explore the entire Puget Sound region. Accommodation and restaurant options range from homey to luxurious and a thriving artist community adds culture to this quiet island. Wildlife is abundant and public golf is available.

Photography by Charles Gurche: Olympic Park, one of the most majestic costal sunsets.

Top: Hummel Lake at sunrise
Photo by Charles Gurche
Bottom: Eagle Fishing
Photo by James T. Jones

Lopez Island: Known as the "Friendly Isle" and the "Jewel of the San Juan Islands," Lopez Island offers rolling farm roads and woodlands that are perfect for biking. A coastline of steep cliffs is interspersed with secluded beaches and coves that make for magical little adventures and love affairs. The island is 15 miles long and 8 miles wide with over 2,100 year round residents.

Orcas Island: Orcas Island is the largest of the islands. Known as the "Gem of the San Juans," it is located in the banana belt of northwest Washington. Orcas enjoys over 260 days of sunshine and receives only about 22 inches of rain per year. The natural features of the island offer a variety of terrain with lush valleys, mountain peaks, and fresh water lakes. The population is diverse and scattered throughout the pastoral, mountain, and marine settings.

Shaw Island: Shaw is not a large island and is unique in having virtually no commercial or tourist-oriented facilities. Roads are mostly inland and afford little access to, or even views of the shoreline. Always a surprise to first-time visitors and ferry-riders, the dock at the Shaw landing is operated by brown-habited Franciscan nuns who also run the adjacent Little Portion store.

Decatur Island: is considered a "private" island, having no public facilities other than a County launching boat ramp in Davis Bay. There are about 59 full-time residents and about 627 potential weekend residents that show up during the summer months. Most of the locals commute by boat to Anacortes for groceries, about a 20 minute trip on a nice day. There is a one room schoolhouse, teaching children from first through eighth grades. The high school students are sent to Lopez by boat.

Seattle "The Emerald City"

Nationally recognized as one of the most livable cities in the United States, Seattle is where you can explore the contrasting thrills of a metropolitan playground on the edge of the wilderness. It's Pike Place Market, Pioneer Square, Seattle Center and Space Needle, ferry rides, art and music, and the best coffee on the planet!

In Seattle, more than anywhere else in the world, the forefront of technology and urban culture stand arm in arm with a dramatic coastline and the high alpine terrain. The climate is decidedly comfortable. Seattle actually gets less rain per year than New York, Chicago, Miami or Atlanta. Winters are mild and summers are perfection, with persistent blue skies and temperatures that make air conditioning unnecessary and enable year-round outdoor activities. Snow is rare downtown, but a number of impressive ski areas, some less than an hour away, receive more of the white stuff than any region on Earth. The mild climate also makes activities like golfing, fishing, whale watching and hiking possible year round.

Founded in 1869, the City of Seattle is located on Puget Sound, 113 miles from the United States and Canadian border. Its first economic boom came in the 1890s, as the last departure point for those chasing the Klondike Gold Rush. It continued to prosper as a major Pacific port with the opening of the Panama Canal in 1914. In 1962, Seattle hosted the World's Fair for which the futuristic Space Needle was built.

Surrounded by mountains and water, the greater Seattle area features picture-perfect views and year-round recreational opportunities. The awesome height of Mt. Rainier, over 200 miles away, is contrasted well as it stands tall above the downtown skyscrapers. For some of the best views of the Seattle skyline, take in a Seattle Mariners baseball game at Safeco Field or a Seattle Seahawks game at Qwest Field. Both venues offer spectacular views of the skyline and majestic coastal sunsets.

Seattle has been ranked as one of the best U.S. cities in which to locate a business and is headquarters to such mega corporations as Boeing, Microsoft and Amazon.com. Boeing is the largest aircraft manufacturer in the world and consistently one of the top three exporters in the United States. Microsoft is the world's leading personal computer software company, but at the same time, just one of 2,500 software development firms in the state. In fact, 76% of Seattle residents have Internet access at home.

Biotechnology also contributes to a healthy economy, as do many large retail employers that include Nordstrom and Costco. Another business that has become an icon of Seattle is Starbucks. This coffee giant not only has cafes both nationally and internationally, but on practically every street corner in the city.

Tourism is Washington State's fourth largest industry. The Norwegian Cruise Line has added Seattle as a homeport and the Washington State Convention and Trade Center completed a major expansion in 2001. The Seattle Center and local hotels have gained a reputation as exciting venues for conferences and conventions. Other major city facilities include the Bell Harbor International Conference Center and a new Stadium Exhibition Center. There are 4,415 hotel rooms in downtown Seattle and 27,901 hotel rooms in the Seattle-King County area. The area's cultural diversity has also produced a wide variety of ethnic restaurants, and Seattle is famous for fresh seafood, local farm produce, and other Northwest specialties.

Photography by:
Martin Bydalek

The Pike Place Market is the soul of Seattle, the oldest continuously operating farmers market in the country. The famed market is a bazaar of fresh seafood, fruit, vegetables, flowers, ethnic eateries and specialty shops amid a menagerie of artists and street performers. The nine-acre historic district hosts nine million visitors each year.

Since 1971, when Starbucks established its first store in Seattle's historic Pike Place market, partners have been welcoming customers in Seattle and around the world.

The Starbucks Support Center, the coffee retailer's global headquarters, is an urban landmark anchoring Seattle's SODO business district.

Photos provided by Starbucks

The district began a slow decline during World War I and was home to the original "Skid Road". This term was used to signify when timber slid down Yesler Way to the waterfront. Preservationists rallied in the 1960s to save the area's exquisite ensemble of Victorian and Edwardian Era architecture and today, Pioneer Square survives as a designated Historic District.

Seattle boasts a large population of artists, supported in part by an innovative public arts funding program. For example, since 1973 it has been a legal requirement that one percent of city capital improvement project funds be spent on artworks. Performances, galleries, museums, concerts, festivals, and attractions offer limitless possibilities to experience art, history and culture.

Seattle has more cultural construction projects in the works than any other urban area in the U.S. Other additions include the new Olympic Sculpture Park on the downtown waterfront (Seattle Art Museum), a new Museum of History and Industry at the expanded Washington State Convention and Trade Center, a new downtown central Library and extensive renovations to the Opera House.

In the shadow of the Space Needle, the monorail runs through the architecture of the *Experience Music Project*, an interactive journey to the soul of rock music. Bars and clubs feature live bands that are constantly renewing the city's reputation as an incubator for powerful new sounds. Washington is the birthplace of both Jimi Hendrix (Seattle) and Bing Crosby (Tacoma) and is one of the few cities in the U.S. to boast a major opera, symphony and ballet company. The Seattle Opera is one of the finest companies in the country, as is the Seattle Symphony, which performs in Benaroya Hall, adjacent to the Seattle Art Museum. Seattle is a center for live theatre, especially small, fringe theatre productions.

Photo provided by EMP

The Experience Music Project (EMP) is a one-of-a-kind music museum that combines interactive and interpretive exhibits to tell the story of American popular music. The outside of the EMP building is as stimulating as what is on the inside. A fusion of textures and a myriad of colors, the museum structure symbolizes the energy and fluidity of music. The final design was influenced by the bright hues of electric guitars.

Peer into tide pools teeming with life or trace a river through a rain forest to its glacial source. Find area restaurants that are always innovating to keep pace with the city itself. Sail the sunsets in solitude, ride a bike on rolling roads, or surf and snowboard in the same day. That's life in Seattle.

Established in 1892, the Seattle Yacht Club is located on Portage Bay in a fresh water bay connecting Lake Union with Lake Washington. The 8500 square foot clubhouse is conducive to warm and friendly gatherings and the formal dining room is one of the best in the Seattle area.

Permanent moorage is provided to members at the Portage Bay main facility and two piers at Elliott Bay. Moorage is also available to members of clubs that provide reciprocal guest moorage.

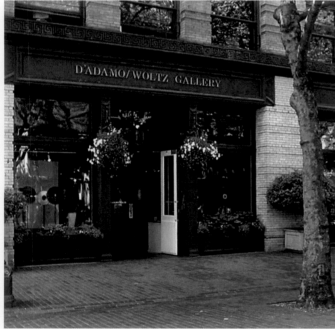

The last stop in the states for gold prospectors heading to Alaska, the waterfront attracts people with its sea air and sounds. A simple Seattle pastime is to stroll the adjacent waterfront or relax and watch the ferries glide to and from the islands. Washington State Ferries depart carrying passengers and cars to Bainbridge Island and the Olympic Peninsula.

Shopping in Seattle rivals most large cities. Small designer boutiques coexist with big retailers. With over 190 art galleries, Seattle offers all aficionados a sensory vacation.

Located in historical Pioneer Square, the D'Adamo/Woltz Gallery presents an ongoing contemporary fine-art collection of regional and international paintings, sculpture and glass. *Photos provided by D'Adamo/Woltz Gallery*

Seattle's skyline as defined by its architecture is a combination of innovation and style. A decade of explosive growth in technology, trade, and communications, has presented tremendous opportunity to design professionals. Take the "Underground Tour" for a unique perspective on the city's cultural history and architectural style. Pioneer Square is Seattle's oldest neighborhood. Most of the Square's buildings were erected within a decade of the disastrous Great Fire of June 6, 1889.

University of Washington

Founded in 1861, the University of Washington (UW) has long been a leading institution of higher learning in the Pacific Northwest. More than 38,000 students study under an internationally respected faculty of almost 3,600 instructors earning degrees in a broad spectrum of programs.

The University of Washington has garnered attention for its landmark work in software development, cancer treatment, and integrated circuit design. Research is complemented by the strong presence of nationally and internationally known corporations at the forefront of new technology. The Boeing Company is a leader in aerospace research. Developers and manufacturers of computer hardware, software and communications equipment are located in Washington, among them Hewlett Packard, Intel, Attachmate and Microsoft. In addition, forest products companies maintain major research facilities in Washington, including Weyerhaeuser and Simpson Timber.

The university also helps shape the cultural identity of the Pacific Northwest through its support of the arts and collegiate athletics.

Photos provided by University of Washington

Faculty and graduates helped launch Seattle's now thriving theatre scene, and the university currently operates three theatres that stage almost 100 performances each year. For sports fans, there are NCAA football games at Husky Stadium and athletic events in 22 additional sports for men and women.

The U.S. News and World Report rank the best graduate schools listed 13 of UW's graduate programs in the top 25 in the nation, including the medicine, dentistry, nursing, public health, and computer science programs.

Founded in 1946, the UW School Of Medicine excels in both scientific research and clinical training for more the 1,500 residents and fellows. With a prestigious faculty of more than 1,600 that includes three recipients of the Nobel Prize, it is consistently among the top five medical schools in both the amount of federal research funding received and in the transfer of technology. The UW Medical Center ranks among the best hospitals in the nation and serves as a referral and treatment center for a wide array of specialized health care needs.

Bellingham: Located on the Bay, the northern edge of Puget Sound, with Mt. Baker as its backdrop, Bellingham is the last major city before the Washington coastline meets the Canadian border. Situated between two of North America's most international cities, Seattle and Vancouver, Bellingham has a spectacular natural environment. This bay side community offers historic districts, antiques, galleries, museums, golf, a farmers market, parks, whale watching, and ferries to the San Juans.

Anacortes: This town is the crown jewel of Fidalgo Island and easternmost of the San Juan Islands. Fidalgo is accessible by bridges from the east and from Whidbey Island to the south. A deep water working port since the early 1900's, Anacortes has a rich maritime history. Century-old buildings and an extensive collection of historical murals decorate the city and the historic downtown area is filled with shops, entertainment and thriving art galleries. Ideally situated within the rain shadow of the Olympic Mountains, Anacortes is a popular spot for camping, kayaking and bicycling.

Edmonds: Located on Puget Sound, gateway to the Olympic Mountains, Edmonds has generated a reputation as Washington's "Friendliest City." Celebrated for its public art and downtown old-time streetlights adorned with hanging flower baskets, Edmonds is most reminiscent of small-town America. The fantastic flowers that line the streets and the fragrant hanging baskets have become a hallmark of this charming, artistic town. Edmonds is only minutes from Seattle with marine, charter boats, fishing pier, beaches, shopping, and waterfront dining.

Mount Vernon: Mount Vernon offers great activities for every season. Located in Skagit County, it is the home of the Skagit Valley Tulip Festival, as well as the Trumpeter Swans that spend the winter just outside the city limits. Skagit Valley College is an award-winning community college that services three counties. There are also many local lakes for fishing, swimming and boating fun. Mount Vernon is a historic riverfront town named "Best Small City in the U.S." in 1997 in the "The New Rating Guide to Life in America's Small Cities".

Everett: An All-America City, and the county seat of one of the fastest-growing counties in the nation. Nestled between the beautiful Cascade Mountain Range to the east, hundreds of forested islands and the oceanic wildlife of the Puget Sound to the west, Everett is consistently rated as one of the best places to live by the national media. Everett is a beautiful bay side city offering Aqua Sox pro baseball, waterfront cruises, golfing, charter fishing, live theatre, art galleries, and the popular Boeing Tour Center.

Kirkland: A suburban city infused with vitality where joggers, shoppers, business people and retiree's all mingle along the boulevard. It's a town where conversation in coffee shops ends at 11 p.m., and then only under protest. The City of Kirkland was named after a British-born steel tycoon, Peter Kirk, who came to the Northwest in the 1880s seeking new development opportunities. Kirk envisioned developing a "Pittsburgh of the West" on the eastern shore of Lake Washington - a bustling new town whose main economy would be focused around steel production.

Redmond: A city known worldwide as a center for high technology. In 1985, Microsoft Corporation, founded in 1975 by Bill Gates and Paul Allen, had outgrown its offices in Bellevue and was looking for a place to set up a corporate campus. They chose Redmond as their headquarters and the rest is history. Redmond is also the "Bicycle capital of the Northwest" featuring the Derby Days Bicycle Race and Derby Days Festival.

Bellevue: This city has evolved from a "bedroom community" into the economic and cultural hub of the Seattle-area's Eastside. Located three miles east of Seattle, Bellevue is about ten miles west of the foothills of the Cascade Mountains. The city has developed its downtown core into a major business and retail center while maintaining the safe, comfortable family neighborhoods for which it has long been popular. Kelsey Creek Park has hiking trails, a playground and a barnyard zoo. The Bellevue Botanical Garden in Wilburton Hill Park offers demonstration gardens and a 1/2 mile trail through native forest, meadow and marsh.

Renton: The city of Renton, located 15 miles southeast of Seattle along the southern shores of Lake Washington, has been a manufacturing center for the Pacific Northwest for more than a century. Probably the largest influence in Renton's success came in 1941, when The Boeing Company moved in and set up shop. During World War II, the Boeing Renton plant was turning out B-29 planes at a peak rate of six per day. Renton is referred to by some as the "Jet Capital Of The World."

Photo provided by Bruce Forster

Photos provided by Museum Of Glass

Museum Of Glass:

The Museum of Glass in Tacoma features contemporary art with a focus on the medium of glass. Visitors feel the heat and see the action as artists create works of glass in the shimmering steel cone that contains the Hot Shop Amphitheater, a working glass studio with amphitheater seats and a catwalk that allows close-up views of the artists at work. Reflecting pools and panoramic views draw visitors to the roof of the Museum of Glass. A must see is Tacoma native Dale Chiluly's 500-foot-long pedestrian bridge leading to the Washington State History Museum.

The Museum of Glass is one of the seven design wonders of the world in 2003 as reported by Conde' Naste Traveler magazine.

Tacoma: Washington State's third largest municipality. Located just 18 miles south of the Seattle-Tacoma ("Sea-Tac") International Airport, Tacoma is easily accessible from Interstate 5. The city offers rich historical districts, cultural activities and numerous visitor attractions. Take that wonderful breath of air at 5,000' along the Wonderland Trail on Mt. Rainier or at dusk cross the incredible Bridge Of Glass. A feeling of relaxed contentment is Tacoma's trademark just as much as Mt. Rainier or the Museum of Glass cone.

The Tacoma Dome is the world's largest wooden domed arena, measuring 530 feet in diameter and standing 152 feet tall. Opening in 1983, the space covers 6.1 acres and was constructed at a cost of $44 million.

There are many different configurations involving the 16,000 movable seats that convert the dome from large stadium events such as football or soccer to arena events such as concerts or ice shows. The Exhibition Hall has 30,000 square feet of space and the arena and the hall together offer 130,000 square feet of meeting space.

One of the best concert facilities in the nation with superb acoustical qualities, the dome has been the venue for entertainers from Bruce Springsteen and Garth Brooks to Frank Sinatra and The Stones. The first concert at the Tacoma Dome was David Bowie, Aug. 11, 1983. The top grossing show was The Rolling Stones, with over $2.4 million in gross receipts on November 6, 2002.

Photo provided by The Tacoma Dome

Olympia: The Capital of Washington State and located at the tip of the Puget Sound about 60 miles south of Seattle. The name reflects the view of the majestic Olympic Mountains. In recent years, Olympia, with its neighbors of Lacey and Tumwater, have witnessed phenomenal growth. Olympia is a splendid capital city with harbor-side boardwalk, farmer's market, forested parks, historic districts, and an opulent state capitol set in spectacular grounds.

Bremerton: Since 1891 Bremerton has been the home of the Puget Sound Naval Shipyard. The Port of Bremerton provides a spectacular natural setting along with a short commuting distance to the urban centers of Seattle and Tacoma. Harbor tours pass the shipyard where the Navy's inactive fleet is moored. Cultural attractions include the Amy Burnett Gallery, the Admiral Theatre, the Bremerton Naval museum, and the Kitsap County Historical Society Museum. Bremerton's annual Armed Forces Festival in May, first celebrated in 1938, is the oldest event of its kind in the country.

Aberdeen: Located in Grays Harbor County, Aberdeen is the home of Washington State's tall ship ambassador, the Lady Washington. The county and bay called Grays Harbor is on the Olympic Peninsula, 49 miles west of Olympia and 109 miles southwest of Seattle. In 1990, the Grays Harbor area and its largest city Aberdeen were singled out from 219 small communities as being one of the ten best "micropolitan" areas in which to live in the United States.

Blaine: Whatcom County's most northwesterly situated town and the busiest border crossing point between British Columbia, Canada and Washington. The Peace Arch State Park spans the US/Canadian border as a monument symbolizing nearly two centuries of peace between the countries. Blaine is also home to the Historic Washington Foot Passenger Ferry that takes tourists across the bay to the Semiahmoo spit, and the Inn at Semiahmoo, a world-class resort community featuring an Arnold Palmer designed championship golf course.

Oak Harbor: Located at the northern tip of Whidbey Island, Oak Harbor offers sweeping views of Puget Sound and the surrounding Cascade and Olympic mountain ranges. Well known for its small town atmosphere and local charm, Oak Harbor is the entryway to Deception Pass State Park with more than 4,000 acres of forest, campsites, trails, breathtaking sunsets and ocean beaches. Named for the many Garry oak trees that grace its skyline, Oak Harbor is the home of the Whidbey Island Naval Air Station.

Port Ludlow: A residential and recreation community built up around the shores of Ludlow Bay. There is a 300-slip marina and side ties for boats up to 200 feet. The premier 27-hole championship course is a golfer's paradise where deer roam, cedar stumps emerge from water hazards and wildflowers explode in a riot of spring colors. The natural environment offers hikes on wooded trails and paths, clams and oysters along the beach, and drives through the scenic countryside.

Port Angeles: Nestled between the Olympic Mountains and the Strait of Juan de Fuca, Port Angeles is the largest city on the North Olympic Peninsula and gateway to Olympic National Park. There are a variety of tour operators and tours available to the traveling public that offer back-country touring, guided-fishing experiences, mountaineering, rafting trips, horseback riding, kayak excursions, or a trip to the top of Hurricane Ridge.

Port Townsend: Historically, Port Townsend was a major seaport in the 1800's and today it is designated a National Historic Landmark. Famous for its Victorian Homes Tour, Wooden Boat and Rhododendron Festivals, the community of Port Townsend is as varied as the geography that surrounds it. From recreation in the Olympic Mountains to drama at the downtown theatre, the reflection of life here is both connected to the land and to the people. Discovery Bay, the Strait of Juan de Fuca and Port Townsend Bay all surround the city as it sits at the northeast end of the Quimper Peninsula.

Vancouver: The community sits on the north bank of the Columbia River directly across from Portland, Oregon. The Pacific Coast is less than 90 miles to the west. The Cascade Mountain Range rises on the east and Mount St. Helens National Volcanic Monument and Mt. Hood are less than two hours away. The spectacular Columbia River Gorge National Scenic Area lies 30 minutes to the east. Vancouver combines the excitement of a major metropolitan area with small-town charm and abundant recreational opportunities. The moderate climate here results in lush forests and abundant foliage and Spring time explodes with blossoming trees and shrubs.

Centralia: Halfway between Seattle to the north and Portland to the south, Centralia is about a one-hour drive from many great day trips and weekend locations. Getting its start as an industrial city with logging and sawmills, the farming of grain, hay, hops and fruit serve as the major commodities. There are a number of antique dealers in historic downtown and fifty factory outlets. Centralia is known as the Gateway to Mount St. Helens and Mt. Rainier.

Friday Harbor: On the East side of San Juan Island is the town of Friday Harbor, also the San Juan County Seat. Friday Harbor is a quaint seaport that rises from the ferry landing and public marina where it is an easy stroll to the docks, airport, parks, restaurants, shops, galleries and lodging facilities. This charming historic fishing village, the largest town in the beautiful San Juan Islands, greets visitors as they arrive by ferry, seaplane, airplane or boat. Once here, it is time to relax and enjoy the romantic inns, wonderful boutiques and art galleries, the harbor-view restaurants, outdoor activities and nature.

Roche Harbor Village: On the north end of San Juan Island is the port of entry known as Roche Harbor Village, a picturesque little town and a favorite anchorage for yachts. Listed on the National Register of Historical Sites, it is approximately ten miles from Friday Harbor. This village will take you back in time to a quiet, relaxed pace as you stroll the beautiful Victorian gardens and enjoy the ambiance of the historical buildings. Roche Harbor has an airstrip, marina, lodging, grocery store, restaurants, shopping and recreational activities.

Gig Harbor: Located at the south end of Puget Sound is the quiet waterfront village of Gig Harbor. This tucked-away town sits on a scenic inlet framing a postcard-perfect view of Mt. Rainier. Gig Harbor's strong Scandinavian and Croatian heritage has always influenced its nautical lifestyle and fishing-village character. Specialty shops, creative boutiques, art galleries and waterfront restaurants add to its appeal and make it a wonderful get-away. Rich in maritime history, scenery, and unparalleled recreation, the Gig Harbor Peninsula area is a haven for scenery lovers and those seeking an escape from the ordinary.

Washington

The North Cascade Range is a towering mass of granite spires and pre-historic glaciers. Amid these jagged peaks, you can walk in the quiet of ancient forests, swim in seas of wildflower and peer into the glass of alpine lakes. Travel through a land full of rolling hills, steep canyons, and historic towns. The Palouse represents idyllic America - a land of amber waves and warm-hearted people. Raft through the deepest canyon or gaze out on a sea of rolling wheat from atop a high butte.

Winthrop

If you travel the North Cascades Scenic Highway, be sure to visit Winthrop, eastern Washington's historic old west town. Located in the Methow Valley at the foot of the Cascade Mountains, Winthrop adopted its old Western theme in 1969. It is believed that Owen Wister may have written portions of the classic novel "The Virginian" while honeymooning here. Golfing, shopping, dining, biking, hiking, mountain climbing, boating, and cross-country skiing are all available along with a live glimpse into the old west.

Lake Chelan

Recognized as one of the premier resort destinations in Washington. It is best known for it's warm sun and clear blue lake. At one end of the lake sits the resort town of Chelan where travelers come to enjoy the endless water and outdoor recreation. At the far end of the lake where mountains soar in excess of 9,000 ft. is the remote village of Stehekin and the North Cascades National Park, accessible only by boat or float plane. Lake Chelan is all about fun. Whether you like high adventure, leisure sports or playing around with the kids, there is something here for everyone.

Wenatchee

Located in the heart of Washington at the confluence of the Wenatchee and Columbia rivers, Wenatchee and the Wenatchee Valley stretch beneath a line of spectacular semiarid mountain ridges. The mountains are high with lush forest and pristine alpine lakes. A fishing and hunting ground for Plateau Indians for thousands of years, the Wenatchee Valley was settled during the 1870's by ranchers, traders and apple growers and today is at the forefront of Washington's apple industry. Climb, ski, hike and mountain bike in the mountains. Fish, kayak, raft and parasail the rivers.

Ellensburg

Home to Central Washington University, Ellensburg hosts travelers visiting the Gorge Amphitheater and Grand Coulee Dam. Ellensburg is a great place to stay for a few days while visiting the Washington Wine Country and the Yakima River, one of the best fly-fishing rivers in the country. Ellensburg is like an oasis with rivers, lakes, streams and mature shade trees on the "dry" side of the Cascade Mountains. This university town features whimsical public art, historic downtown buildings, art galleries, museums, and rodeos.

Opposite page: Green Mountain Glacier Peak Wilderness.
Below left: Columbia River Gorge.
Photos by Charles Gurche

Washington's Scenic Highway

THE SKAGIT VALLEY

WHIDBEY & FIDALGO ISLAND

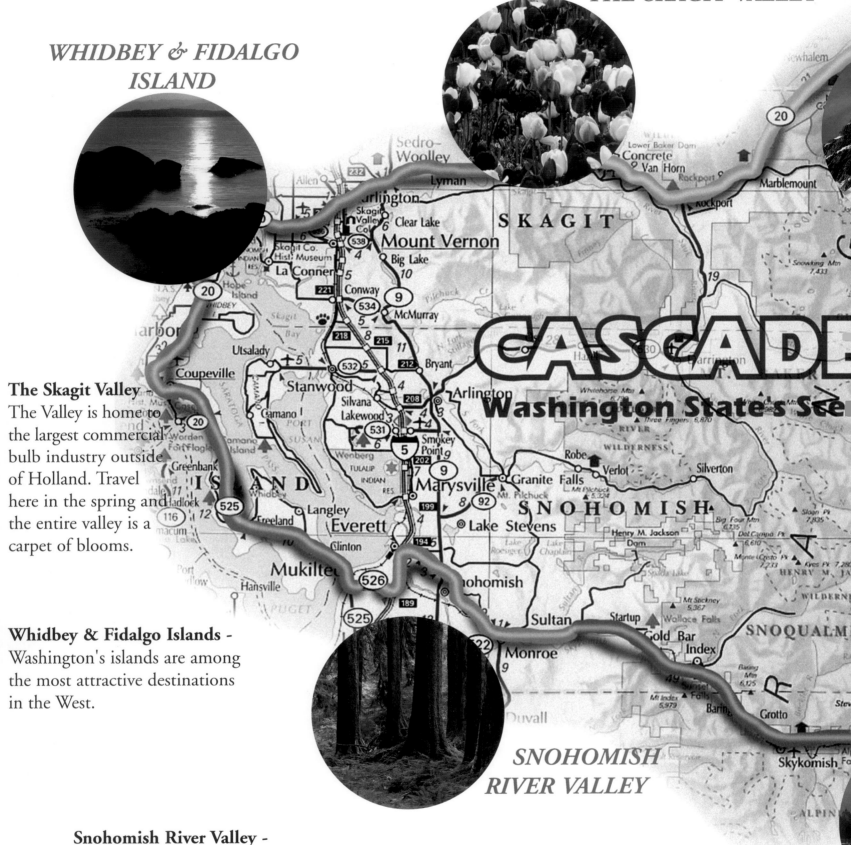

The Skagit Valley
The Valley is home to the largest commercial bulb industry outside of Holland. Travel here in the spring and the entire valley is a carpet of blooms.

Whidbey & Fidalgo Islands -
Washington's islands are among the most attractive destinations in the West.

SNOHOMISH RIVER VALLEY

Snohomish River Valley -
The Cascade Loop begins at sea level in the bustling port city of Everett, just 28 miles north of Seattle.

STEVENS PASS

Stevens Pass -
At the crest of Stevens Pass, you will see sweeping views of the forested country. As you cross the Cascades, you move from the wet, lush, maritime climate to the drier open woodlands of the east slope.

Washington offers many scenic drives filled with majestic views of nature. The spectacular scenery ranges from dense rain forests to rugged mountain summits, with rolling farmlands and regal forests. The scenic routes allow drivers to enjoy great views, fascinating wildlife, and a wide range of outdoor activities.

The Cascade Loop is a 440-mile self-guided driving tour from the waters of Puget Sound, across the Cascade Mountains to the vast, sun-baked orchards of the Columbia River Plateau. Take a day-trip or travel the entire Loop and take your time. While an average trip can take between 2-4 days, you could spend forever exploring the intricacies of the Loop. The Cascade Loop showcases nine separate regions, each with their own distinct personality.

North Cascades -
The grandeur of the Cascade Range will entertain you with waterfalls, alpine meadows, mountain lakes and magnificent timber.

Methow Valley -
The Methow Valley is Washington's equivalent of the Old West and is famous for its superb stream and lake trout fishing.

Lake Chelan -
Abundant sunshine and winter activities make Lake Chelan a popular year round destination.

Cascade Foothills -
In the Cascade Foothills you will find the Bavarian Village of Leavenworth, nestled tight up against mountains that rise to more than 8,000 feet.

The Columbia River -
This area is more than a gorgeous natural wonder. The river is arguably the most significant environmental force in the Pacific Northwest.

NORTH CASCADES

METHOW VALLEY

LAKE CHELAN

CASCADE FOOTHILLS

THE COLUMBIA RIVER

History

The spectacular scenery of Central Washington ranges from rugged mountain summits to rolling farmlands, regal forests and steep cliffs. Amidst the natural grandeur are the historic towns that welcome travelers with reminders of our history and the early pioneers. Two miles west of Stevenson, is the site of a portage where hardened visionaries reassembled their wagons after rafting down the river from The Dalles, Oregon.

The wildlife is plentiful along the many streams destined for the Columbia River.

Visit in the spring when the valley blossoms with its annual parade of glorious flowers back-dropped by dramatic views of Mt. Baker and the Cascade Mountains.

Maryhill Museum of Art - Klickitat County In 1907, Samuel Hill, a wealthy entrepreneur bought 6,000 acres of land overlooking the Columbia River. He chose the bluff that Maryhill Museum now occupies as the site for his own home. The museum serves as a nature conservancy as well as a place to experience art. Just south of Goldendale, Hill built an authentic replica of England's famous Neolithic Stonehenge and dedicated the monument to the servicemen of Klickitat County who died during World War I.

Leavenworth

In the early 1960's, the leaders of the community decided to change Leavenworth's appearance. Using the beautiful backdrop of the surrounding Alpine hills to their advantage, the town remodeled their hamlet in the form of a Bavarian village. Today, more than a million tourists come to Leavenworth each year, each visitor finding their own individual love affair with the community. Washington's "Bavarian Village" offers spectacular scenery, year-round recreation activities, authentic German food, unique shops, and great accommodations.

Amid these jagged peaks, you can walk in the quiet of ancient forests, swim in a sea of wildflowers and peer into the glass of alpine lakes. Since changing to a Bavarian motif, Leavenworth has become a pillar of the tourism industry in the Pacific Northwest. Today, more than a million tourists come to Leavenworth each year.

Moses Lake

Home to one of the state's largest natural fresh water lakes, plus numerous parks and campgrounds, Moses Lake is an outdoor recreational oasis! Experience free summer concerts, seasonal Saturday Farmers Market, and Washington's premier family aquatic center. The lake on which the town lies is made up of three main arms that are over 18 miles long and up to one mile wide. Moses Lake has over 120 miles of shoreline, covers 6,500 acres, and offers year-round recreational activities.

Grand Coulee Dam

The 8th Wonder of the World and North America's largest concrete structure, The Grand Coulee Dam stands as a monumental achievement of the determination, success and risks of the thousands who contributed to its creation. The dam is the largest concrete dam in North America and the 3rd largest producer of electricity in the world. Total concrete used to create the dam was 11,975,521 cubic yards. Home to the world's largest laser light show, you can see it nightly from Memorial weekend through September.

The Tri Cities

With hundreds of sunny days, the Tri-Cities offer plenty of opportunities to play in the great outdoors. Play a round of golf, stroll through one of the beautiful parks, bike, hike or roller blade the Sacagawea Heritage Trail.

Kennewick

The first home to the Chemnapum Indians, the name means "Winter Haven," an appropriate title as the tribe gathered in the mild climate to trade, fish and pasture their horses. Kennewick is the largest of the three cities and relies on light industry and retail to support their thriving economy. The history includes that of "Kennewick Man," a 9,200 year-old skeleton unearthed in Kennewick's Columbia Park. Here you will find specialty shopping, WHL hockey, a water park, historical museum, Audubon nature trail, great golf, organic wines, and a family fishing pond.

Pasco

A city near the site where the Lewis & Clark Expedition made camp in 1805. The expedition spent several days near present-day Sacajawea State Park trading with the Indians and cataloging the diverse plant and animal life. Pasco has both strong agricultural and industrial roots and is the largest city in the million-acre Columbia Basin Irrigation Project. A farmer's market, factory outlets, Sacajawea State Park, historical museum, McNary Wildlife Refuge, WBL baseball, golf, wineries, breweries and a new railroad museum are all part of the Pasco experience.

Richland

Known for starting out as a small farming community, and then the population boomed from about 1,500 to more than 51,000 residents in 1943 when the government built the country's first nuclear reactor on the Hanford Site. The Hanford Site continues to play a major role in the Tri-Cities economy and is also a huge part of the science and technology communities worldwide. Richland is home to historical and children's museums, two science centers, great golf, beautiful parks, numerous wineries, and water sports.

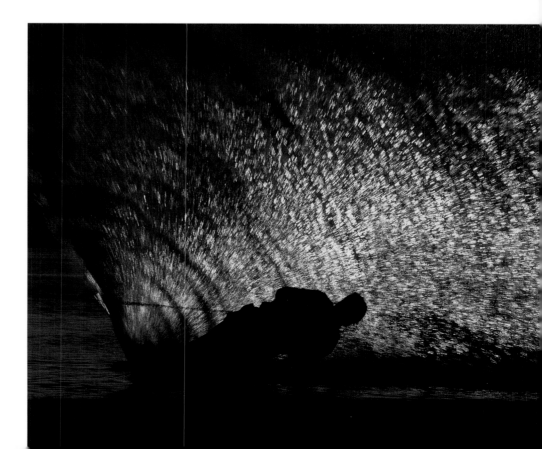

Our beautiful Columbia Gorge!!

Columbia Gorge, Photo by: Ron Keebler

"Green Douglas firs where the waters cut through, down her wild mountains and canyons she flew. Canadian Northwest to the ocean so blue, it's roll on, Columbia, roll on. Roll on, Columbia, roll on. Roll on, Columbia roll on. Your power is turning our darkness to dawn, so roll on Columbia, roll on."

"Roll on Columbia" the official Washington State folksong, written by Woody Guthrie in the spring of 1941

People have lived along the Columbia River for more than 10,000 years, making it one the most historically significant environmental features in the state. Here is where you will find the haunting cries of Sandhill cranes and the midnight calls of the coyote.

Raft through the deepest canyon or gaze out on a sea of rolling wheat from atop a high butte. Whether you choose to fish in the shadows of the towering mountain peaks or ski on the glassy surface of a sun-soaked lake, Central Washington is a year-round recreational outdoor paradise.

Here is where you can ride on rolling roads or windsurf and snowboard in the same day; hike through vast tracts of coniferous forests and search for the last herd of wild caribou. If you bike on the peaceful farm roads or lay tracks on virgin winter powder, keep your camera handy. The experiences are unlimited.

Stevenson

An historic river town and the county seat of Skamania County. The southern border of the county is defined by the Columbia River Gorge National Scenic Area while the northern territory holds the peak of Mount St. Helens in the west and the base of Mt. Adams to the east. Two miles west of Stevenson was the site of a portage where pioneers reassembled their wagons after rafting down the river from The Dalles, Oregon. Stevenson offers the new Skamania Lodge, the Columbia River Gorge Interpretive Center, gift shops, and art galleries.

Wine Country

As you cross the Cascade Mountain Range from the west on your way to southeastern Washington, you emerge from the forest into the dry, rippling hills of Wine Country. The days here are warm, the nights are cool and, to the joy of winemakers, the latitudes are about the same as Burgundy and Bordeaux in France. In this agricultural paradise where the sun shines more than 300 days a year, the rich volcanic soils and warm, desert-like climate present ideal growing conditions for local vintners.

Large-scale irrigation, fueled by runoff from the melting snowcaps of the Cascade Mountains, has unlocked the dormant potential of the volcanic soils. The extra-long growing season, controlled irrigation, and the entrepreneurial spirit of the winemakers are producing trellises laden with rich grape varietals that are sending signals to the world about Washington wine. The production of Washington wines has more than doubled over the past decade with prized harvests of award winning labels.

With special events that take place year round, the wineries offer an open invitation to enjoy the solitude while you peer out over an oasis of orchards and vineyards, and experience one of the state's best kept secrets... Washington Wine Country.

Yakima

The Yakima Valley receives 300 days of sunshine each year and offers year-round recreational opportunities. Less than 200 miles from Seattle, Spokane and Portland, the close proximity to the Puget Sound and Portland areas makes this charming valley irresistible. The Yakima Valley's abundance of recreational activities includes a "PGA" 18 hole golf course, great shopping and a variety of tours, museums, and antique shops. Experience sun, wine, gourmet dining, affordable lodging, fresh fruits and vegetables in season, museums, antique and specialty shopping.

Photo provided by the Yakima Valley Winery and Washington Wine Association.

Washington

The northeast region of Washington, known as the Rocky Mountain Gateway, is still unspoiled with vast tracts of coniferous forest and dense mountain terrain.

The southeast region is a major wheat producer, chiefly in the hilly Palouse area, a land of amber waves and warm-hearted people.

Spokane

Located along the eastern border of Washington, Spokane is the largest city between Seattle and Minneapolis on the I-90 corridor. Spokane is four-season country, each contributing to the region's unique lifestyle. The topography of the land varies from rolling wheat fields to snow-capped mountains, from lush forests to deserts, and from pristine lakes to raging rivers.

Cheney

Home to Turnbull Wildlife Refuge and Eastern Washington University, Cheney offers small-town charm only 17 minutes from downtown Spokane. With four distinct but mild climate seasons, sports and recreational opportunities thrive in Cheney. Popular outdoor activities include fishing, boating and swimming at several nearby lakes.

Pullman

Home of Washington State University and located in southeastern Washington's rolling wheat fields, Pullman has much to offer visitors, students and those seeking a lifestyle that combines a beautiful country setting with the benefits of a major university.

Clarkston

The Gateway to Hells Canyon and because of the year-round warm weather and mild winters, the area is often referred to as the "Banana Belt." Located at the confluence of the Snake and Clearwater rivers and surrounded by gentle rolling hills, the Lewis-Clark Valley is at the head of the navigation system of the Columbia and Snake Rivers.

Walla Walla

Steeped in history and set against the backdrop of the Blue Mountains, you will be pleasantly surprised at what Walla Walla has to offer. The name is of Indian origin and means " many waters". The historic Nez Perce Trail was located where Main Street is today and the Lewis & Clark expedition skirted the northern and western boundaries of the Walla Walla Valley in 1805.

Opposite page: Wenatchee River, Wenatchee National Forest.
Right bottom: Ice coated trees, Spokane County
Photos by: Charles Gurche

53

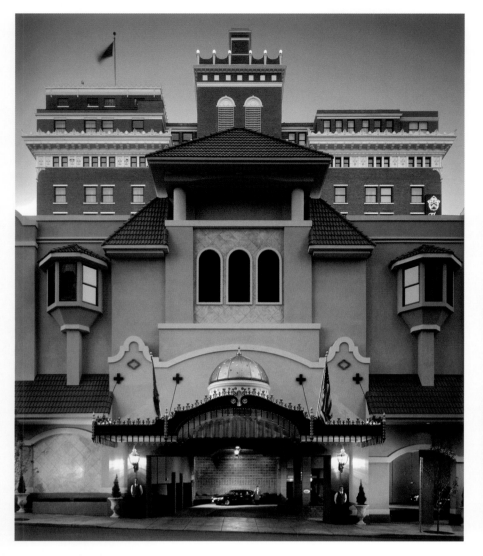

The Davenport Hotel

The hotel opened in 1914 at a cost of $3 million, which was a million dollars over the projected cost. It was a masterpiece of the time and its guest list has included dignitaries from around the world. Today, The Davenport Hotel has 283 spacious guestrooms, including 24 suites and retains all the amenities of luxury and elegance.

Commercial real estate developer Walt Worthy and his wife, Karen, bought the empty landmark in 2000 and began the massive restoration process. They kept most of the popular public spaces, such as the ornate lobby, gilded ballrooms and the Hall of Doges, modeled after the Doges Palace in Venice. The second-floor ballroom, surrounded by medieval arches and lighted by a crystal candelabrum, was lifted in one section and stored during renovation, then reinstalled beside the new 6500-square-foot grand ballroom.

Restored to its old glory, but with an appeal to the modern business and vacation traveler, the magnificent and historic Davenport Hotel is a sight to behold. Located in downtown Spokane, the hotel offers first class accommodations, conference facilities and restaurants.

Photos provided by Peter Hassel and
The Davenport Hotel

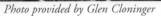
Photo provided by Glen Cloninger

Kirtland Cutter Projects in Spokane

Kirkland Kelsey Cutter was Spokane's principal architect from 1888 to 1923. To Spokane, he contributed the Davenport Hotel as well as a number of mansions for Spokane's elite.

Cutter (1860-1939) grew up in Ohio and after studying art in New York and Europe, traveled to Spokane in 1886. Despite his lack of professional education in the field, Cutter was determined to become an architect. His designs cover a wide variety of styles, from the rustic and picturesque to the formal and classical. Some of the works in Spokane designed by this beloved and respected architect include: Patsy Clark, Glover Mansion, Spokane Club, Monroe Street Bridge, Amasa B. Campbell House, Wakefield House and Finch House.

Credited with rebuilding the city of Spokane after a devastating fire, he came to architecture from an interest in illustration. Cutter's exquisite interior spaces suggest his background in the arts.

Photo provided by Glen Cloninger

Gonzaga University is a private, four-year comprehensive university. Located in Spokane, Gonzaga's campus is situated on 108 acres along the beautiful Spokane River, within a 10-minute walk of downtown Spokane.

Gonzaga is named after a young 16th century Italian Jesuit, Aloysius Gonzaga, who died in Rome trying to save young people from the plague. He was later named the patron saint of youth. "Cura personalis", or care for the individual, is the guiding theme of the university.

Photo provided by Gonzaga University

The power of Spokane Falls roars right in the middle of the city, in harmony with the world-class Spokane Symphony Orchestra that recently celebrated 50 years of outstanding performances. Nowhere else in the world is such a large waterfall part of the downtown urban landscape.

The Great Northern Clock Tower lies at the center of Riverfront Park. The Clock face is 9 feet on each side, making it the largest Clock Tower in the West.

When the Riverfront Park was constructed for Expo 1974, the train station was demolished leaving only the Clock Tower.

Spokane Indians Baseball Team
The Spokane Indians are the Class A affiliate of the Texas Rangers operating in the NW League. Games are played at the 7,000 seat Avista Stadium at the Spokane Fair & Expo Center.

Photo provided by Spokane Indians

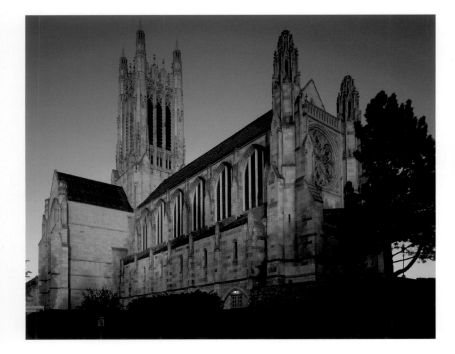

Saint John's Cathedral

The Cathedral suggests the typical English Gothic Cathedral, but the construction detail includes French influence. The structure is solid masonry with exterior stone quarried near Tacoma. The interior of the nave is sandstone from Idaho and the remainder of the interior is stone from Indiana.

Ponderosa Pine Country

If you want to escape to the backcountry, where humans are only guests, the emerald stands of Colville National Forest comprise an amazing 1.1 million acres of protected forestlands. Fir-covered peaks over 7,000 feet tall and hundreds of miles of trails access the Selkirk Mountains, Kettle River Range, and the precious old-growth forests of the Salmo-Priest Wilderness.

Winter sport enthusiasts can spice up the cold months with a variety of snow activities. Cross-country and downhill skiing, ski-boarding, snowmobiling, snowshoeing and tubing are available at a variety of locations.

Washington State University

This University is one of the largest residential campuses west of the Mississippi. A multi-campus research institution, WSU offers a liberal arts education balanced with practical instruction in professional and technical fields. Students on the Pullman campus are provided strong career preparation and academic support programs in a small town living environment conducive to academic achievement.

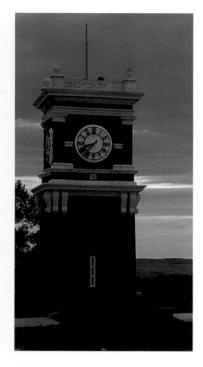

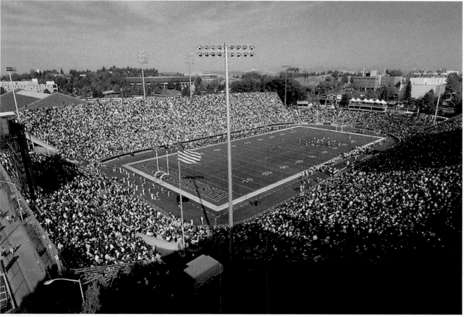

Visitors are invited to explore WSU's extensive campus and soak in the beautiful architecture, blending both classic and contemporary styles. Afterward, enjoy a fine meal in one of Pullman's many restaurants ranging from authentic Mexican to Szchewan Chinese. Of course, steak and seafood are always a Palouse favorite.

Photos provided by Washington State University

Biking, fishing, and watching the wildlife

Travel over the gentle rolling hills and rural farmlands of Eastern Washington on a warm summer evening and experience a plethora of shapes and colors that will forever inspire the imagination. The landscapes of the Palouse Hills and the grassy ridgelines that make this part of Washington unique are sprinkled throughout with barns of every shape and size, some weathered by time and others freshly painted.

The rich black soil and ancient silt deposits from the Ice Age make the wheat harvests plentiful. Catch the golden shades of the wide-open countryside and watch wild animals in their element. Green in the spring and golden in the summer, a great view of the region is from the top of 3,613 foot high Steptoe Butte near the Idaho border.

The Palouse and Walla Walla Annual Balloon Stampede

With the richest soil on the planet, the Palouse is one of the most productive wheat-growing regions in the world.

The Palouse is rich in history, dating back more than 10,000 years to the first Native Americans. Lewis and Clark passed through nearly two centuries ago on their journey to the mouth of the Columbia.

The Palouse is far more than just picturesque farm country. Raft down the Snake River through Hells Canyon, the deepest gorge in North America and explore the wilderness of the 1.4 million-acre Umatilla National Forest with its rugged backcountry of peaks and canyons.

Washington

Resorts, Golf Courses & Mountain Ski Areas

RESORTS

Rosario Resort and Spa
Orcas Island, Washington

Salish Lodge & Spa
Snoqualmie, Washington

Sun Mountain Lodge
Winthrop, Washington

Skamania Lodge
Stevenson, Washington

Roche Harbor
Roche Harbor, Washington

Alderbrook Resort & Spa
Union, Washington

GOLF COURSES

Broadmoor Golf Club

Members Club at Aldarra

Gold Mountain Golf Course

Skamania Lodge

Royal Oaks Country Club

Newcastle Golf Club

Desert Canyon Golf Course

TPC Snoqualmie Ridge

Sahalee Country Club

Washington National

Indian Canyon Golf Club

SKI AREAS

Crystal Mountain
Western Washington Area

Mount Baker
Western Washington Area

Mission Ridge
Central Washington Area

Stevens Pass
Central Washington Area

63

Located on beautiful Orcas Island in the Northwest corner of Washington, Rosario was built in 1906 and fully renovated in 1997. As a result of the renovation, all of the hotel's rooms are five-star quality and most have scenic water views.

1-800-562-8820
WWW.ROCKRESORTS.COM

ORCAS ISLAND, WASHINGTON

Sprawled along 30 acres of waterfront property, Rosario offers convenient access to outdoor recreation, including biking, sightseeing, and whale watching. The health and beauty spa has 3 pools, a work-out room, sauna, Jacuzzi and a host of pampering and rejuvenating spa treatments and services. With 127 guest rooms and suites that offer fireplaces, sunken Jacuzzi tubs, private balconies and spectacular views of the Cascade Bay and Marina, you will find Rosario to be a great setting for romantic weekends, personal retreats and family getaways.

With an elegant historic mansion as its focal point and enough activities and amenities to keep you busy for a week's vacation, Rosario is a premier resort in the San Juan Islands.

Rosario's conference center is equipped to handle groups from 20-400 with a choice of intimate, elegant, business and event settings. When you include the natural beauty of the San Juan Islands, add the luxurious health and beauty spa and activities such as whale watching, hiking, cycling, kayaking, snorkeling and scuba diving, you will agree that Rosario Resort & Spa is the ideal retreat.

SALISH
LODGE & SPA

1-800-272-5474 / WWW.SALISHLODGE.COM

Escape to romance and relaxation amidst a mountain paradise. Sip the clear air as you wind down from an awakening trek to the base of Snoqualmie Falls. Bathe in the warmth of the fire as you sink down into your whirlpool tub.

SNOQUALMIE, WASHINGTON

One of Washington's premier resorts, Salish Lodge & Spa is located just 30-minutes east of Seattle. This elegant escape nestled in nature features all the finest amenities of a luxury hotel. The local rivers and crystal clear lakes provide ample opportunity for rafting, kayaking, eagle watching, fishing, mountain biking and much more.

The Salish Indians considered the area a very magical place. One visit will confirm their belief as you listen to the roar of Snoqualmie Falls while whitewater tumbles over the granite cliffs and falls nearly 300 feet into the emerald river canyon below.

While you may come to get lost in the natural beauty of Snoqualmie Falls, you'll want to stay for the luxury of the elegant lodge and spa. Here you will find the best of both worlds .... a rare combination of outdoor magic and indoor comfort that makes for a unique mountain experience.

SUN MOUNTAIN LODGE

Located near Winthrop, high in the Cascade Mountains of north-central Washington, Sun Mountain Lodge has become one of the Northwest's finest four season resorts. Spring through Fall, Sun Mountain Lodge offers a wide range of activities and every season reveals new outdoor experiences just waiting to be discovered.

1-509-996-2211 / WWW.SUNMOUNTAINLODGE.COM

WINTHROP, WASHINGTON

There are over 100 miles of trails for hiking while mountain biking and horseback riding, fly-fishing, river rafting, canoeing, tennis, and golf are all available. During the powder season, the lodge turns into a winter wonderland where you can glide onto the second largest cross-country ski trail system in the United States or go for a sleigh ride and let the horses do the work. Either way, the hot pools and spa will be awaiting your return.

Some folks come simply for the views and to watch the stars glimmer over the Cascade Mountains while they dine on gourmet delicacies or quietly savor the tranquility of the sunset from their own private balcony. Like the views, Sun Mountain's award-winning menus change with the seasons.

*S*et on 3,000 acres, Sun Mountain's unique combination of privacy, tranquility and serenity make this resort a "must visit". Whether you're here to quietly remove yourself from the routine or try your hand at a long list of activities, the folks at Sun Mountain Lodge invite you to discover the sublime high above the Methow Valley.

Sun Mountain Lodge offers a rare combination of luxury and nature unparalleled in a four-season resort. Anytime is a good time to visit the "Resort For All Seasons."

DOLCE Conference & Resort Destinations™

1-800-221-7117 / WWW.DOLCE.COM

Located by Stevenson, Washington, Skamania Lodge reflects the unique Northwest style architecture that carefully blends into the natural surroundings of the Columbia River Gorge. This rustic mountain retreat boasts the most spectacular vistas of any hotel in the Gorge.

STEVENSON, WASHINGTON

Skamania Lodge is the only golf resort in the area with an 18-hole course. Enhanced by the area's natural beauty, the course features a driving range, putting and chipping greens, practice bunker and full-service pro shop. Challenging as well as breathtaking, the course winds through the forest and around ponds, taking full advantage of the natural landscape. Spectacular vistas from the elevated greens and the towering Douglas Firs make this course a joy to play.

Although golf is the preferred sport, Skamania makes the ideal base for Gorge exploration and is recognized as one of the region's most popular adventure destinations for white water rafting, windsurfing, horseback riding, mountain-biking and hiking. Two outdoor tennis courts, a sand volleyball court, and over four miles of hiking, fitness and bike trails are also part of this beautiful property.

Washington Resorts

*L*ocated along Lewis and Clark's historic trail and surrounded by waterfalls, peaks, forests and canyons, the recently expanded 254 guestroom hotel and 22,000 square-foot conference wing make planning a meeting a pleasure for corporate and association events.

Regional cuisine and wines are featured in the restaurant along with the spectacular vistas. Dine in splendor overlooking an incredible view of the Columbia River Gorge and Cascade Mountain Range and relax in the warmth of the lodge while enjoying some of the most spectacular scenic views in the world. Native American culture is represented through-out the lodge by rugs, original stone rubbings and warm Pendleton fabrics.

Enjoy the sunsets on the outdoor sun deck and find yourself surrounded by fragrant wildflowers. A tasteful blend of luxury amidst nature, this rustic yet pristine mountain resort and conference destination has become known as one of the region's most popular adventure destinations.

On the north end of San Juan Island, nestled in a beautiful protected bay, is the port of entry known as Roche Harbor. With its historical ambiance and quaint seaside village charm, Roche Harbor is a perfect year-round destination, averaging 247 days of sunshine each year and half the rainfall of Seattle. While most of the island is pastoral, you will find expanses of forests, rocky cliffs and small mountains around Roche Harbor.

1-800-451-8910
WWW.ROCHEHARBOR.COM

ROCHE HARBOR, WASHINGTON

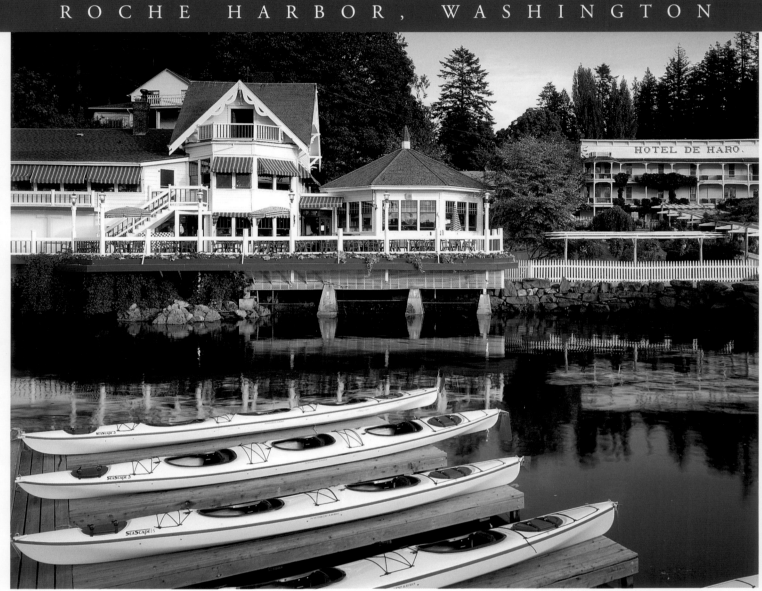

Photo by Charles Gurche

Roche Harbor will take you back in time to a quiet, relaxed pace as you stroll the beautiful Victorian gardens and enjoy the ambiance of the historical buildings. Listed on the National Register of Historical Sites, the village is approximately ten miles from Friday Harbor, the only town on San Jaun Island.

A popular destination for boaters, in 1997 new docks and slips were added to the marina and it now accommodates over 370 vessels. If you are traveling by private boat, a friendly dockhand will help you moor your vessel upon arrival.

For lodging try the historic Hotel de Haro built in 1886, the McMillin Suites overlooking the harbor or the cottages located near the swimming pool and beach.

Whether you are coming by private boat and docking in the marina, flying in and landing at the airstrip, or traveling by ferry as most people do, you will marvel at both the journey and the destination.

Surrounded by outer islands, it is in these protected waters that an abundance of wildlife can be seen.

ALDERBROOK
RESORT & SPA

1-800-622-9370 / WWW.ALDERBROOKRESORT.COM

Originally opened in 1913, Alderbrook Resort & Spa is experiencing a new generation of luxury. After nearly two years of extensive renovation and re-created in 4 star luxury, Alderbrook is one of the Northwest's premier destinations for both leisure travelers and conference retreat planners.

UNION, WASHINGTON

*A*lderbrook is located just west of Seattle on the Hood Canal, a natural, glacier-carved fjord more than 60 miles long. The canal's pristine water is world renown for scuba diving and rich abundance of sea life. Curiously unique, the shores are encrusted in oysters, the docks lined with mussels and the sea teems with salmon.

Photo by Martin Bylachek

Photo by Martin Bylachek

Washington Resorts

Inspired by its magnificent natural setting and colorful history, Alderbrook conveys a sense of harmony with its surroundings. What remains from the renovation are the spectacular views of the Olympic peaks, the glistening waters of Hood Canal, and the surrounding landscape of Alder, Evergreen and Cedar trees. The new Alderbrook is an excellent compliment to the natural beauty of the surrounding landscape.

For those wishing to experience the romance and beauty of the Hood Canal, Alderbrook features a full-service spa and fitness center, waterfront restaurant and bar, fully equipped hi-tech meeting and banquet space, 77 guestrooms and 16 cottages.

The hotel and guest accommodations are inspired by the beauty of the outdoors. The interior, presented by Dawson Design, captivates people on an emotional level, through finishing colors of sage green, by emphasizing the lush landscape, the chocolate brown of the surrounding Olympic Mountains and the vibrant reds of a rewarding sunset. You are guaranteed to find one of the most scenic wilderness areas on earth.

Photos by: David Phelps

UNIQUE Golf Courses of

WASHINGTON

Broadmoor Golf Club - Seattle, WA

Golfers in Washington enjoy some of the world's most diverse and dramatic vistas as they travel the fairways in pursuit of their passion. The natural terrain of the state yields an impressive array of styles and conditions.

Many famous designers have used Washington's natural landscapes to create world-class courses. The Golf Club at Newcastle, designed by renowned golf course architect Robert E. Cupp, offers dramatic views of Mt. Rainier, Lake Washington and the Seattle skyline. Some courses, like the Gold Coast Olympic, are sculpted into the splendor of the Pacific Northwest.

Members Club at Aldarra - Fall City, WA

Skamania Lodge - Stevenson, WA

Gold Mountain Golf Course - Bremerton, WA

Photo: hole 16, Rob Perry

Royal Oaks Country Club - Vancouver, WA

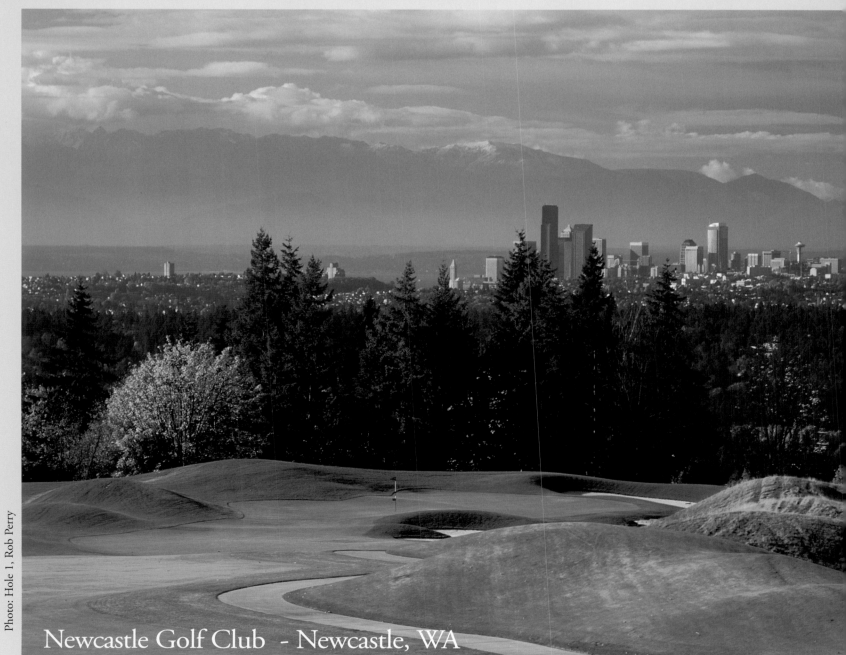

Photo: Hole 1, Rob Perry

Newcastle Golf Club - Newcastle, WA

Desert Canyon - Orondo, WA

The entire state of Washington is an exotic golf destination with a diverse line-up of top courses. Try the challenge of tight tree-lined fairways or desert golf with deep ravines and wastelands. Play the wooded enclaves, rolling terrain and wide fairways. Enjoy the vistas from elevated greens that showcase the splendor of the Columbia River Gorge. Play PGA Championship courses that treat the golfer to a variety of playing challenges and stunning panoramic views.

TPC Snoqualmie Ridge - Snoqualmie, WA

Sahalee Country Club - Sammamish, WA

Photo: Hole 1, Rob Perry

Photo: Hole 16, Rob Perry

Courses in Western Washington are open year-round because of the relatively mild weather. Courses in Central and Eastern Washington typically start to close down in the Fall and re-open in the Spring with the exception of the Tri-Cities area in South-Eastern Washington, where because of the "banana belt" climate, courses here stay open year-round.

Washington National - Auburn, WA

Photo: Larry Conboy

Indian Canyon - Spokane, WA

Mountain Ski Areas

WASHINGTON

Mt. Baker - Western Washington

Photos by: Scott Wicklund

Photos by: Scott Wicklund

Stevens Pass - Central Washington

*W*ashington is gifted with skiing unsurpassed in accessibility and variety of terrain. The Summit at Snoqualmie and Alpental together offer four mountains within an hour of Seattle.

Bring your snowboard to surf the fabled terrain park of **Mt. Baker**. This glaciated volcano is the birthplace of snowboarding. Both skiers and snowboarders love the mountain for its diverse terrain, unspoiled by crowds.

Stevens Pass is the most popular ski and boarding destination in Washington. It offers trails spanning all degrees of difficulty, including the incredible backside of the mountain that is one of the premier terrain parks in the world.

At **Crystal Mountain**, rated one of the top 25 ski areas in the country by Skiing Magazine, take a ride up the "Rainier Express" for a close encounter with the massive, glaciated face of Mt. Rainier. The immensity of this mountain, with a vertical rise similar to Mt. Everest, is something you will not believe until you see it for yourself. Many ski areas brag about high-speed quad lifts, well, at Crystal, two 6-person, high-speed chairs will whisk you to the top of the mountain faster than a line can form at the base.

Photos by: Scott Wicklund

Photos by: Snowdragon Adventure shots

Crystal Mountain - Western Washington

Photos by: Snowdragon Adventure shots

Mission Ridge is just a few hours from Seattle, near Wenatchee on the eastern face of the Cascades. The snow is deep and light, but the terrain is steep and challenging. Although the majority of the runs are more difficult to expert, there's plenty of terrain for all ability levels.

No matter where you ski in Washington, lift lines are luxuriously short and lift tickets are reasonable. For cross-country enthusiasts, the Methow Valley in North Central Washington is legendary.

Photos by: Scott Wicklund

Mission Ridge - Central Washington

The Evergreen State is one of the most diverse areas the United States has to offer. In a single day one can experience majestic mountains, dense rain forests, desert vistas, volcanic splendor, fertile fields of fruits and flowers, an inland sea, a maze of island wonderlands, coastal beaches, and the largest metropolitan area in the Northwestern United States.

Within these wonderfully diverse locations exist some of the most unique homes found anywhere in the world; homes that are as varied as the settings they are found in. In this section of the book you will see both the mesmerizing views of the exterior architecture and locations themselves, as well as the unbelievable beauty and exquisite individualism of their interior spaces, including homes in excess of 27,000 square feet, mansions, high-rise condominiums, beach cottages, and even yachts.

Publisher:
RhinoBooks
www.rhinobooks.net

WESTERN

First Hill Living in Seattle, Rainbow Rock Residence, The House at Semiahmoo, The MV Olympus Yacht, Livable Art at Pike's Peak, The Lute Residence, In Harmony with Puget Sound, Lady Lola Yacht, Gig Harbor Retreat, The Rietz Residence, Fabulous Alki Point Condo, Smith Tower Penthouse, North Bend Estate, Knight Residence, Cozy on Bainbridge Island, The End of the Rainbow, Fanch Retreat at Wing Point, Lime Kilm Residence.

CENTRAL

The DeAtley Residence, Snyder's Snug Harbor.

EASTERN

The Brett Residence, Double River Ranch, The House at Eagle Bluff, Higashi Resideance.

Unique Homes of
Washington

First Hill
in Seattle

Photography by Michael Mathers

First Hill has the distinction of being Seattle's oldest residential neighborhood. First Hill Plaza is considered one of the most prestigious condominium properties in Seattle. Truly in-city living at its finest. The views from this 28th floor home are as spectacular as they come. Sweeping vistas of the city scape, Puget Sound, Lake Union, the Olympic and Cascade Mountains, and fabulous Mt. Baker make the glow of day or the twinkling of evening lights even more amazing.

ARCHITECT: SANDLER ARCHITECTS – SEATTLE, WA
BUILDER: JAS DESIGN-BUILD, INC. – SEATTLE, WA
INTERIOR DESIGNER: ELISABETH BEERS – SEATTLE, WA

This three-bedroom, three-bath condominium features beautiful marble, limestone and granite floors, and the most stunning custom cabinet woodwork found anywhere. The patterned Pommele Sapele dark wood adds an unusual richness to the space and blends well with the abundant light from the high Northwestern exposure.

Tibetan rugs, European artwork, and an exquisite African sculpture showcased on a Philippian Mulava wood roller lends a pleasurable, artistic, and international flair to the main living areas. High-rise living has a style all its own and is unique to each owner's taste. When combined with the condominium's resort style amenities, such as a swimming pool, exercise facilities, entertainment and guest facilities, and 24-hour security, this living style offers all the creature comforts of home as well as the conveniences of city life.

Comfortable surroundings, Tylek paintings, deep rich woods, and fabulous views make this home the ideal environment. Add to this a personal sauna, steam shower, and high-tech entertainment system, and it is difficult to find a reason to want to go elsewhere.

Comfortable elegance is the term that best describes this wonderful home built near the ninth green on a golf course located just a few miles south of the U.S. and Canadian border.

BLAINE, WASHINGTON

Photography by Michael Mathers

W hen the owners set out to design their Pacific Northwest dream home, their vision was a home that soaked up the exquisite beauty of towering trees and invited the sun to warm their home and hearts. They wanted a home that truly flowed with the environment. The tall cedars and soaring eagles of Semiahmoo provided the perfect setting.

Having long admired the work of Frank Lloyd Wright, they wanted the outside of the house to bear his trademarks of large overhangs, windows without headers and soffits that flowed into the interior. Lots of light and open spaces were also a priority, as evidenced by ceilings ranging from 10 to 23 feet high.

ARCHITECT: TREVOR EULEY DESIGN STUDIO – VANCOUVER, B.C.
BUILDER: SAND DOLLAR MANAGEMENT COMPANY, – BLAINE, WA

The home exudes the natural beauty of wood and features solid cherry interior doors, custom milled woodwork, and accentuated highlights such as the hand built arch over the entry door shown.

The House at
Semiahmoo

*T*he beautiful kitchen is sized to accommodate large parties. The custom crafted cabinets are furniture grade and the countertops are solid slab granite with double beveled edges. The overall kitchen design is reminiscent of a French country château. Indirect lighting was used above the cabinets to accentuate different levels and heights of cabinetry. The dining room adjoins the kitchen, overlooking the garden and lake and will seat 14 people.

The floors throughout this warm and elegant home are Turkish Travertine with design inserts of tumbled marble.

The custom wooden windows have low E Italian azure blue double window glass to protect the furniture from fading and provide warmth to the sky on cloudy days. Interesting ceiling detail is used to cloak indirect lighting in the main living area.

The master bedroom is a spacious retreat overlooking the lake of the 9th green on the golf course. The ceiling is 10 feet high with indirect lighting concealed in a circular cove.

The Gem of Seattle
The MV Olympus

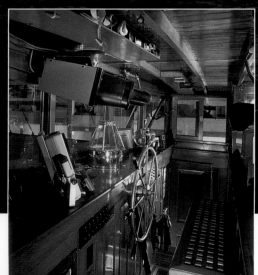

SEATTLE, WASHINGTON

Photography by Alonso Rochin

This 97 foot, twin diesel, fantail yacht was originally built in 1929 for the president of the New York Stock Exchange. The MV Olympus combines beautiful old world craftsmanship and new world comfort to provide a nostalgic retreat on one of the most elegant yachts remaining from the 1920's era.

The MV Olympus has a rich tradition and history. She has been host to dignitaries and celebrities over the years, ranging from President Truman in her earlier days, to Senator Warren Magnuson, Julie Andrews, Robin Williams, and Governor Gary Locke in more recent times. The yacht even displays the original guest log with President Truman signing his address as "temporarily 1600 Pennsylvania Avenue". The yacht was taken by the U.S. Government during WW II to serve as a navy vessel. After the war, it was purchased as "war surplus" by the State of Washington in the 1940's and refurbished into the "Governor's Yacht". It became a major item of controversy when the public discovered that over $100,000 was spent on refitting her, consequently costing Governor Mon Wallgren his re-election and causing the yacht to be promptly sold by the newly elected Governor.

BUILDER: NEW YORK YACHT, LAUNCH & ENGINE CO. – NEW YORK
OWNERS: DIANE & JOHN VAN DERBEEK – SEATTLE, WA
CAPTAIN: SCOTT GIENOW – SEATTLE, WA

The yacht has been privately owned and operated since 1949. The boat's current owners, John and Diane VanDerbeek, performed a complete interior renovation in 2000, restoring the grand old lady to her original luxury and condition. The boat continues to play a prominent role in the life of the City of Seattle, is often used to lead the yacht parade for the Opening Day of Boating each spring, and also serves on special occasions as the "unofficial" Governor's Yacht.

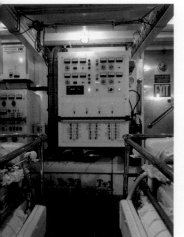

he main salon is elegantly furnished. The formal dining area seats eight, while the fantail can comfortably accommodate twelve for formal luncheons or dinners. The fantail can also be open or closed as desired. Four handsomely decorated staterooms have their own private entry baths. The exquisite use of brass, teak and oak provides all those aboard with an experience that has been described as "gliding along in a stately manner". This yacht is truly a gem and the pride of Seattle.

95

Livable Art
at Pike's Peak

BELLEVUE, WASHINGTON

Photography by Michael Mathers

This custom home is a modern masterpiece wherein the architectural design, modern interior art, beautiful furnishings, and interior design all melt into one. The home is a perfect blend of Art Deco, Mediterranean elegance, and modern design; making it both a home and a work of art. Meticulous attention to detail and creative use of space are prevalent throughout the home.

The unique art coves built into the walls utilize distinctive spot lighting to highlight attractive glass-art and sculptures. The glass-art etched double entry doors lead to a rotunda of elegant columns with curving walls & ceilings in the entry area. This home provides many intriguing designs and styles around every turn.

ARCHITECT: AKHAVAN ARCHITECTURE – LOS GATOS, CA
BUILDER: THOMPSON RESIDENTIAL DEVELOPMENT – BELLEVUE, WA
INTERIOR DESIGNER: SALLY A. THOMPSON – BELLEVUE, WA

Nestled in the private wooded hills of Bellevue, Washington, this 4,420 square foot home has spacious 17 and 12 foot ceilings in key living areas with abundant sunlight throughout. Extensive use of marble, granite, and rich hardwood flooring, along with the custom hand blown glass sinks nestled in granite, surround visitors in beauty wherever they turn. The use of custom glass countertops, shelving and accent pieces, along with curved slab granite in the kitchen and wet bar, present stunning displays of artistry that flow well with the other areas in the home. The 1,800 square feet of granite and marble variations include rare cobalt chip and Brazilian plum. The overall impact of the interior design and decoration is absolutely stunning.

The freeform blend of function and design is evident everywhere in this home. The theme is also prevalent outside with the pool, waterfalls, spa, cabana, raised seating area, built in BBQ, and sports court area. "Livable Art" is a very appropriate description of this classy, tranquil and pleasant environment.

Lute Residence

R I C H M O N D   B E A C H ,   W A S H I N G T O N

Photography by Steven Young

Located in Richmond Beach, the Lute residence is a home of history and renovation. The Kerry family (of Kerry Park fame) commissioned architect Paul Thiry in the 1930's to design side-by-side summer homes on their seven-acre estate in this waterfront community by the Puget Sound shoreline.

Thiry, the principal architect for the 1962 World's Fair gained fame for his introduction of European modernism to the Pacific Northwest and was responsible for some of Seattle's most prominent public buildings of the 1950's and 1960's.

ARCHITECT: PAUL THIRY — SEATTLE, WA
INTERIOR DESIGN: CYNTHIA LUTE — RICHMOND BEACH, WA

Top left: A private terrace.
Center right: A grapevine provides cover for the arbor.
Bottom left: The study.
Bottom right: The kitchen.

*W*hen the Lutes purchased the property 60 years later, both homes and the property were in disrepair. Years of uncontrolled growth had consumed the garden areas, but with careful pruning, the landscape reveals mature fig trees, pear trees, camellias and roses.

Top right: A living room chaise
frames the view into the dining room.
Center left: Bathroom vanity is topped
with a 19th century Italian mirror.
Below: The top floor of the tower.

Today, the property is a showcase of the Lute's passion for
renovation. Although the two houses are only 10 feet apart,
a 14-foot change in elevation separates them. Mrs. Lute
commissioned architect Norman Yelin for the challenge and
today a corrugated steel tower links the two homes. Public
spaces comprise the upper home while the lower remains
private family quarters.

In Harmony with Puget Sound

MUKILTEO, WASHINGTON

Photography by Michael Mathers

Designed to respect nature and blend with the environment, this astonishing home is the perfect compliment to its surroundings. Designed by Taliesin West Architects, a subsidiary of the Frank Lloyd Wright Foundation, Windintide is one of the few truly environmentally friendly, "green" homes in the state of Washington. It complies with all state energy codes and is the tightest custom-site-built home on local record.

The repeated curved fin design creates a relaxed rhythm and structure for the continuous band of skylights located between the fins. The skylights provide a unique ventilation system to cool the home and also allow for a well-lit, openness to the interior spaces.

ARCHITECT: TALIESIN WEST ARCHITECTS - STEPHEN NEMTIN, SCOTTSDALE, AZ
BUILDER: SHIREY CONTRACTING - ISSAQUAH, WA

The round openings and curves are a continuous theme throughout the house, and even appear in the detailing of the artfully designed kitchen cabinets. Opposite page: A large circular bronze sculpture, Solar Wind, is centered in the circular opening of the first fin.

*D*eep, rich Brazilian cherry flooring helps to emphasize the naturalness and warmth of the home. Great care was taken to ensure the furnishings matched the artistry and natural surroundings. The home instills a sense of peace, beauty and a love of nature.

The deep blue waters of Puget Sound are visible from every room. The cantilevered terrace wraps around both wings of the house to further enhance the fabulous views.

Lady Lola

SEATTLE, WASHINGTON

uane and Lola Hagadone created their idea of the perfect yacht, with all the amenities of home and built for 'around-the-world travel'. The "Lady Lola" is a 68.4 meter, four level, floating marvel that includes one complete upper deck for the owners' personal use, four guest suites, two dining rooms, a captain's suite, 7 crew cabins, a heated swimming pool, two saloons, study, two tender boats with miscellaneous water toys, observation/media lounge, gaming area, bar, Steinway grand piano, lots of sun lounging areas, leading edge technology control room, galley, six machine laundry, and bullet proof glass. The two and a half year project, built by Oceanco under the direction of the Hagadones, produced a very unique residence that cruises at twelve knots, with a range of 4500 nm, to virtually any port in the world.

The highest priority was for an entire upper deck to be devoted to a spacious and comfortable owners' living area with a 180-degree panoramic view. Lola worked closely with the interior designer, Francois Zuretti, to formulate a design masterstroke that combined materials that promote formality and relaxation, as well as brightness and space, yet has the feel of the livable comforts of home. Furnishings, carpeting and white interior all combine with class and solemnity, accented by a magnificent band of dark apple mahogany ringing the lower walls. The warm and subtle texture of Norwegian birch burl round out an absolutely stunning visual effect in every well-proportioned space throughout the yacht.

BUILDER: OCEANCO/2002, MONACO
INTERIOR DESIGNER: ZURETTI INTERIOR DESIGNERS
CAPTAIN: STAN ANTRIM - SAN DIEGO, CALIFORNIA

The custom features of the yacht are too numerous to display them all, but include such unique features as: privacy system for the owners' areas, illuminated panels of sculpted glass, marble floored hallways and bathrooms, a mirrored panel that slides seamlessly hides the stairs to the owners' deck, and glass waterfalls.

*W*indows and mirrors are positioned to allow all 12 seated at the dining table to partake of the magnificent ocean views, while a table for two in the owners' area converts to a table for eight from an ingenious overhead drop down mechanism with the flip of a switch. Lady Lola also features a small discreet serving hatch to the owners' area, fitted wardrobes and drawers, custom tailored dressing room with glass fronted drawers, private communications center, and oh so much more. It even includes, amazingly enough, an 18 hole floating golf course (closest to the pin rules and tour specification floating golf balls). Duane and Lola have managed to make the need for land obsolete.

Gig Harbor Retreat

GIG HARBOR, WASHINGTON

Exterior & Interior Photography by David Papazian. Aerial Photography by Aerolist Photographers, Inc.

The quiet waterfront village of Gig Harbor is nestled at the south end of Puget Sound on the small bay across from Tacoma. The community is rich in maritime history and is one of the most picturesque small cities in America. The Gig Harbor Peninsula area is a haven for scenery lovers and those seeking an escape from the ordinary. It is here on the sandy beach peninsula where you will find this secluded 37 acre retreat.

Set in the middle of towering evergreens, the estate and home were designed for outdoor entertaining and feature stamped concrete patios, ironwood decking, and conversation seating sprinkled amidst 4 acres of landscaping.

INTERIOR DESIGNER: JEFF NAGEL — MONTANA

This home's unique location on the peninsula offers breathtaking sunsets, spectacular views of the Puget Sound waterways and a magnificent "50 yard line view" of Mt. Rainier in its full glory.

Built in 2001, the 7,300 square foot home has the master suite and living areas on the main level. The master suite features an Aspen granite fireplace with tumbled marble throughout the master bath, a full cedar walk-in closet, and a stamped concrete patio with sunken hot tub.

The ceiling heights average ten feet and the walls of windows in the living room and throughout maximize the spectacular views. Electronic sensors adjust the skylights to keep the home light and bright, even on cloudy days.

The gourmet kitchen offers a baker's station, window bar seats and island seating. The formal dining area and large outdoor deck off the kitchen provide the perfect setting for entertaining.

Nature trails meander throughout the 37 acres of mature Pacific Northwest timber, leading to peaceful open meadows. Two ponds stocked with rainbow trout are accented by beautiful waterfalls and a year round creek that completes the serene ambiance of this magnificent estate.

With the shoreline and deepwater bay at the front porch, the owners enjoy beach bonfires, fresh clams and oysters, fishing, beach combing and just plain relaxing in the seclusion of this waterfront community that was originally discovered by those seeking shelter from the storm.

The Ritez Residence

NORTH BEND, WASHINGTON

Photography by Steven Young

North Bend is situated at the entrance to the Cascade Mountains and at the base of Mount Si. The vision the local residents put forth is one of preservation and enhancement. The community wants to preserve its rural character, natural beauty and small town scale. That is what we found in this beautiful North Bend home with its organic inspiration that connects family and home to the mountain setting.

The challenge for architect Christopher Rost was to design a home using a combination of contemporary, rustic, and Japanese architectural influences within a prairie-style home. The result is that no one style dominates the others. The home reflects low, horizontal lines that blend with the landscape while the interior focuses on open space instead of strictly defined rooms.

ARCHITECT: CHRISTOPHER ROST – CALIFORNIA

his 4,600 square-foot home offers views from nearly every vantage point. Wood ceiling beams are used like latticework and showcase the linear, low profile design of the house. The sliding glass doors offer an easy and delicate access to the sheltered patio area.

The role of the garden plays an important part in blending the natural landscape with the home. The lines of the garden seem to merge with the landscape, both serving as the total embodiment of one to the other. Every aspect of the landscape is, in itself, a garden.

*T*he master bath shares a fireplace with the adjoining bathroom. The Montana ledge stone fireplace and the glass bay windows offer the perfect setting for mood music. In a typical prairie home design, the structure is built around a central chimney and offers broad open spaces instead of strictly defined rooms. A good example of this principle is found in the great room that features an open floor plan that joins the living room with the kitchen area.

True to community vision, the home preserves and enhances the goals of North Bend.

Fabulous
Alki Point
Condo

WEST SEATTLE, WASHINGTON

Photography by Michael Mathers

This Puget Sound hideaway offers a contemporary and casual atmosphere with unique design elements. This residence emphasizes an open floor plan with few physical transitions segmenting this 4,300 square foot, single floor dwelling. The design theme reflects the owners' sophisticated, yet casual lifestyle.

Expansive views of Elliott Bay and the Olympic mountains provide an ever-changing mural for this waterside urban getaway. Within the solid concrete and steel building frame reside the rare finishes, expertly crafted fixtures, and technological surprises of modern architecture at its finest. Imported lava counter tops capture the icy-blue hue of northern alpine lakes and stacked slate cuttings form walls of variegated texture and color. Venetian plaster skims interior vertical surfaces and translucent mosaics shimmer against the water features of the in-home spa. Central to the living space is a rotating 60 inch HDTV plasma monitor with THX surround sound.

ARCHITECT: GGLO – SEATTLE, WA
BUILDER: KREKOW JENNINGS, INC. – SEATTLE, WA

Reflective glass tiles clad the columns that have been encircled by decorative cast glass shelving.

Custom cabinetry of Anigre veneer blends well with islands and counters of vivid turquoise lava stone and black concrete. A rolling dining table with pistachio-tinted sycamore top creates a flexible dining experience and enhances the pleasurable color schemes in the adjoining areas. Floating lit glass ceiling panels by artist Jerry Newcomb create a rich and welcoming entryway.

The curving hallway leading to the spa is flanked by a richly textured stone wall on one side and a beautifully crafted plaster wall on the other.

*he bed in the master bedroom
sits graciously against a wall of
Sapele veneers and hidden storage.*

*The 4,305 square foot home
includes a spa, steam bath and
combination gym/guest room,
complete with heated floors.
The eight foot steel tub with the
perfect profile for a reclining
occupant is located next to a basalt wall of water that provides a shimmer
and relaxing ambiance. Translucent glass walled sinks combined with
iridescent mosaic tile and variegated slate to highlight the steam bath
area. The selection of materials throughout the home is very rich in
texture and color, collectively giving one the feeling of being surrounded
by beauty and peaceful serenity.*

The Brett Residence

Photography by Michael Mathers

This Spokane area mansion, nearly a century old, has best been described as a "timeless classic". Originally built in 1917 for T.J. Humbird an executive for the Weyerhauser Company, this seven bedroom, seven bath, 20,000 square foot home transcends its years and remains a remarkably livable, contemporary home with a great deal of grace and functionality. In 1937, Mr. and Mrs. George Jewett took possession and owned it until eight years ago, when Bobbie and Kathy Brett became the third owners of this amazingly resilient old mansion. Other than the recent creation of a wine cellar and remodeling the kitchen, master bath and servants' quarters, remarkably few things have been altered in this wonderful home.

The home's history is steeped in elegance and sophistication. The house is the last mansion created in the Pacific Northwest by architect Kirkland Cutter. The exterior is a traditional Tudor Revival, while the interior is a style described as Southern Colonial Revival. The home features large rooms, well-proportioned spaces, French doors, and many leaded windows to ensure lots of light. A feeling of southern comfort is imparted throughout the home. In days of old, the home was run with a full staff of maids, cooks, butlers, and gardeners. The current owners' influence has brought a more family oriented, relaxed style of living. The Bretts are the owners of the three primary sports teams in Spokane and the sports emphasis is evidenced in the home, although subtle enough to maintain the superb elegance of the original style.

ARCHITECT: ORIGINAL - KIRKLAND CUTTER - SEATTLE, WASHINGTON
BUILDER & REMODEL: PAT JEPPESEN - SPOKANE, WASHINGTON

The home was a model of future technology when built, incorporating such modern conveniences as gas jets in the fireplaces, a gas heated clothes dryer, and even an in-wall vacuum system throughout the home.

Opposite page: From the original 1908 Brunswick bowling alley in the basement to the third floor 200 capacity ballroom, the home is truly a classic. The home has evolved from a formal showplace to a warm and comfortable family style home with a great deal of class and style that maintains the integrity of the original design.

The impeccable landscaping is accredited to the Olmstead brothers, whose accomplishments include such landmarks as Central Park in New York and the grounds of the Boston Commons.

A sports court and natural rock pond with waterfall have been added recently, all of which help to enhance the beauty and enjoyment of the grounds that overlook downtown Spokane, with a northern panoramic view of the valley and Mt. Spokane.

127

The entry way was designed to mimic the grand lodge at Glacier National Park. It features two cedar trees that have 60-inch bases. The massive hand carved mahogany doors present a truly impressive sight to all who enter.

WALLA WALLA, WASHINGTON

Photography by Roger Wade

This magnificent 13,000 square foot home is located in Walla Walla, Washington, the "Napa Valley" of the Pacific Northwest. A great deal of care and planning went into the building of this home over a period of four years. The end result includes everything imaginable, including a 22 car underground garage, in a structure that is rustic, masculine in nature, and possesses a great deal of class. The exterior is a well-blended mixture of Adirondack lodges, Gothic cathedrals, English Tudor styling, and a French Chateau.

ARCHITECT: JON R. SAYLER – SPOKANE VALLEY, WA
BUILDER: DKS CONSTRUCTION SERVICES – WALLA WALLA, WA
INTERIOR DESIGNER: DEBBIE SHAFFER – WALLA WALLA, WA

The Double River
Ranch Residence

*T*he interior construction incorporates a mixture of log post-and-beam with the more traditional framed construction and does a wonderful job of hiding functional necessities such as heating and cooling vents. Australian cypress hardwood tops the floors in the home, while inlaid slate adds color and character to the foyer. Timberline Lodge on Oregon's Mount Hood inspired many of the home's wooden carvings and details. The turret shaped in-home office is accessed from the main structure via a glass-enclosed covered bridge and is heated by a natural wood-burning fireplace.

The open kitchen presents views to the other rooms and promotes a cozy, warm feeling throughout the primary living areas. The massive interior spaces required that everything involving the interior design and decorating had to blend with the space to ensure a comfortable family style of living. Architect Jon Sayler and Interior Designer Debbie Shaffer created a style they refer to as "North Idaho Gothic".

*T*he rear of the home looks out on a spacious swimming pool that enhances the grounds. The views include the luscious valleys of southeastern Washington and the Blue Mountain range in Washington and Oregon.

A poolside cottage includes a sauna, BBQ, recreational area, and also serves as a guest house.

The House at
Eagle Bluff

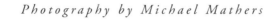

Photography by Michael Mathers

This gorgeous, contemporary home has style that can best be described as "timeless elegance". Nestled in the wooded foothills of Spokane, Washington, this home appears to be an eruption from the earth that simply belongs there among the natural beauty.

The setting presents a feeling of private serenity and the wonders of Mother Nature. All of the stonework utilizes stone and rock natural to the inland Northwest.

The mountainous terrain and rivers in the surrounding area offers some of the best rafting and hiking opportunities in the Pacific Northwest.

ARCHITECT: JON R. SAYLER – SPOKANE VALLEY, WA
BUILDER: DANIEL J. OLSON CONSTRUCTION – SPOKANE, WA
INTERIOR DESIGNER: MARA NEWLUN, R. ALAN BROWN – SPOKANE VALLEY, WA

133

The interior possesses incredible lighting that is very subtle and provides an atmosphere that is extremely warm and comfortable. A wonderful combination of decorating styles and colors, unique open fireplace, and extensive use of granite and straight grain ash throughout the home, blend nicely to create space that is distinctly family oriented, yet elegant in nature.

The grounds emphasize the natural surrounding beauty, highlighted by ponds and impressive landscaping. The family orientation is evident in the groomed baseball area, putting green and tennis court.

The owner took great care to make the guest areas in the home special and inviting, as shown here with the custom glass sink and breathtaking view of the surrounding wilderness in the guest bath.

The
DeAtley
Residence

Photography by Steve Young

This fabulous home gives new meaning to the term "custom built". Every detail was meticulously planned out under the careful guidance of renowned architect Vassos M. Demetriou. This masterpiece took four years from start to finish and involved numerous trips to England, Italy and China to select the perfect materials.

Al and Pat DeAtley have always enjoyed the grand homes of Europe with their high ceilings, tall windows and old world charm. With that influence being the predominant theme, they envisioned a home that could be used not only by the family, but also by the community for philanthropic causes. Carved over the main entrance there is a subtle inscription in Latin: *Non Nabis Solum,* meaning *Not Only for Us.*

ARCHITECT & INTERIOR ARCHITECT:
DEMETRIOU ARCHITECTS – KIRKLAND, WA
BUILDER: KEN MILLER – REDMOND, WA
INTERIOR DESIGNER:
SHOPKEEPER – YAKIMA, WA

This is a home with elegant spaces, superb old world design, detail and craftsmanship. The family space for entertaining, both indoors and out, are inviting and spacious, invoking the tradition of old Europe.

This 27,000 square foot home overlooks the Yakima Valley with the Cascade Mountains as a backdrop. The grounds are exquisite, complete with stately fountains, cascading waterfalls, infinity edged pools and a greenhouse from England. Excellent uses of mahogany and cherry wood, along with burl panels, that create rooms which emit elegance, comfort and charm. The state of the art film screening room is modeled after an early 1920's movie theater, complete with stage for live productions, pool table, bar, and hidden drop-down overhead projector.

No wood was used on the exterior of the building, from the slate roof, and stucco and carved stone walls, down to the extensive use of perfectly level pavers designed to keep the exterior areas dry in summer and winter.

The unique wood burning pizza oven was so massive it had to be installed using a crane.

Snyder's Snug
Harbor

S T E V E N S O N ,   W A S H I N G T O N

Photography by Michael Mathers

This home was created with a great deal of loving care and attention. Much of the wood throughout the home has over a 100 year history, beginning its evolution as the timbers used in the building of the mighty Bonneville Dam. Thousands of hours went into the recovery, reclamation and refinishing that gives the wood its distinctive distressed appearance.

Located in the magnificent Columbia River Gorge, 60 miles east of Vancouver, Washington, this home provides both unsurpassed scenic beauty and the serenity of a woodland retreat. The blooming of the foliage and flowers in the spring is a sight to behold. The unique design, wonderful art, and gorgeous river views makes this home a rewarding treat in all respects.

ARCHITECT & BUILDER: NEIL KELLY-DESIGNERS /REMODELERS.- PORTLAND, OR
INTERIOR DESIGN: JANE SNYDER – STEVENSON, WA

Mr. and Mrs. Snyder helped make Snug Harbor what it is today. When the Washington State road crew was faced with the dilemma of what to do with the huge rocks that were being unearthed, the Snyders arranged to absorb the cost of transporting and lining the harbor with these massive boulders.

*T*he fireplace was a custom design constructed using Colorado lead stone with a liberal sprinkling of petrified wood from the Snug Harbor area. A deer hoof print can be seen in the petrified wood that is to the left of the firebox. Glass countertops are an engineering marvel that required untold hours of research and careful fabrication. Back lighting uses fiber optics and a very intricate chipped edge treatment to further diffuse the light emitted from the sculpted glass edges.

The home takes advantage of a geothermal heating system that extracts heat for this large home from the earth and is four times more efficient than conventional electric heating. An elaborate heat recovery system hidden in the walls uses outgoing air to heat incoming air and provides a heat recovery efficiency approaching 90 percent.

The dock extends out over the river to help capture the ever changing and magnificent views presented by the Columbia River Gorge.

Smith Tower
Penthouse

SEATTLE, WASHINGTON

Photography by Steve Keating

Seattle's historic Smith Tower opened in 1914 enhancing the city's reputation at the time by being the tallest office building in the world outside of New York. At the top of the 522 foot skyscraper is a pyramid shaped Gothic cap that today is one of the most visible residences in the city. Originally housing a 15,000 gallon water tank and used as an adjoining caretaker's apartment, the three-story triangular top on Smith Tower was leased and completely renovated in 1998 by Petra Franklin and now serves as home for Petra and husband, David Lahaie.

After workers disassembled the water tank, Petra hired architect Jim Castanes who removed the ceiling of the existing apartment, creating 1,800 square-feet of living space within the two-story loft. The ceiling in the living area extends the interior view and climbs 45 feet into the beams that support the tower and provide the base for the sphere. Petra replaced the water tank with a Dale Chihuly blue glass chandelier, its colors similar to the beacon light of the tower, and covered the concrete floors with maple. Remaining are the original metal catwalk that was used to service the water tank, the bronze framed arrowhead shaped windows with views of the city and the spiral staircase that leads to the glass dome crowning the building. The views from the home are beyond compare and offer a never-ending panorama of the Seattle cityscape and Puget Sound.

ARCHITECT: JIM CASTANES – SEATTLE, WA
BUILDER: LYMAN CORNELIUS SMITH (1914), – SEATTLE, WA
INTERIOR DESIGNER: PETRA FRANKLIN – SEATTLE, WA

The interior furnishings are a collection of found objects and fine art. Petra salvaged many decorative elements from the building's extensive renovation.

The kitchen countertop resting on top of the antique carved Chinese panels is a result of quick recognition, as workers were on their way to discarding the huge slab of marble. The kitchen shelves display Bauer pitchers and hand-blown glass goblets.

Collectibles line the stairway leading to the main floor and the wood polychrome doors framing the entrance to the bedroom were original gifts given to L.C. Smith from the Empress of China. Glance out from one of the many low dormer windows that surround the living area and watch cruise ships arrive and depart at the Port of Seattle or the roof of Safeco Field as it opens and closes for Mariners games. Best of all, are the sunsets and rises and the city lights at night.

The bright beacon light on the extreme tip of the penthouse helped guide mariners in the early days. One of the first things Petra did before moving in was to change the white beacon lights to blue. Not so extreme it turns out, as the early pioneers favored colored lights as well.

A ladder leads to the 42nd-story and the top of the building where the beacon shines at night. Inside the glass globe, the view again stimulates imaginations that are only restricted by the self. The visions are enormous as you watch trains disappear into the Burlington Northern Tunnel and re-emerge 2 miles later in Belltown or airplanes as they approach Boeing Field. Anyway you look at it, the view is always grand from the top!

North Bend
Estate

N O R T H   B E N D ,   W A S H I N G T O N

Photography by Michael Mathers

Settled at the foot of Mount Si, with its magnificent rural scenery and beautiful Snoqualmie Falls, the Snoqualmie Valley is home to the city of North Bend and an English country mansion where even Shakespeare would feel at home. This elegant estate is precisely crafted and carved within 18 acres of wooded landscapes and gardens, adding a new dimension to luxury and setting an industry standard for craftsmanship.

Architect Robert E. Swain, working in close harmony with the owners, spent many quiet hours simply soaking in the sounds and "listening" for the perfect building site. With 2,000 feet of riverfront solitude available, they uncovered the ideal setting.

Cobblestones from Belgium surround the home on the eastern and western approaches and provide a link to the spectacular flowering gardens, the creek, and the lily pad pond. The Chinese slate roof provides an ideal blend with the Quartzidic limestone blocks, while the copper trim and finely crafted cedar serve to highlight the soft hues and symmetrical images of the exterior.

The front doorbell provides a stately welcome and is fashioned after the original Old English knobs of the 16th Century. This signal for admission will take you back to Windsor Castle, remind you of Big Ben, and prepare you for the wondrous surprises that await inside.

ARCHITECT: ROBERT DESON SWAIN — SEATTLE, WA
BUILDER: JAMES STRODE CONSTRUCTION — WA
INTERIOR DESIGN: DOUG RASAR — BELLEVUE, WA

The extensive use of water featured in the landscape creates a continuous flow throughout the grounds. The reflective pool draws the eye to the river.

The wine cellar, accessed through a hidden panel door from the first floor entryway, includes a vaulted ceiling and sipping area.

*T*he gourmet chef will take special delight in the massive greatroom kitchen. Here you will find a sixteen-foot limestone counter complimented by a twelve-foot "flower counter" that provides continual color throughout the year. The log and lattice hanging area offers easy access to and a commanding showcase of the cookware.

The display of hardwood floors and custom pine cabinetry seems to be an appropriate use of Northwest woods. Choose to gaze from the bay window seating area, relax by the Rumford fireplace, or find yourself setting in the dining room facing out to the light filtered forest.

All elements in the home are carefully designed to reflect the tradition and history of the classic English estate. The library features Madrona wood with a coffered ceiling and burl panels. As you wander through time, the eye uncovers the intricacies and attention to detail. The inlaid maple and mahogany floor of the library is complimented by a custom-made coal basket resting beside the limestone fireplace.

Drawing inspiration from the land, they selected a combination of magnificent stone and copper for the exterior to give credence to the strength and beauty of the home.

The exterior water system provides a unifying theme as it bisects the flower gardens, spills into the water gardens, and flows through the natural vegetation into the creek.

To reach the custom hot tub, follow the Indian tunnel over sea grass mats, exiting through the Rube Goldberg door to the gardens outside. Or traverse the loggia from the master bedroom to the secluded grotto. Either way, the tub will be waiting, with dark green tiles and heated waterfall.

The home is an invitation to savor those precious moments shared by loved ones and friends. On many warm summer nights, the music salon has reverberated with the sounds of fine music.

The Higashi Residence

Photography by Charles Gurche

Cheney, Washington enjoys a small town atmosphere, is only 17 miles to the major metro area of Spokane and is home to the Turnbull Wildlife Refuge, Eastern Washington University, and the Higashi residence featured here.

When Craig and Romana Higashi started the design phase of their home, they requested a unique and carefree low maintenance exterior that would blend with the natural landscape colors of the existing basalt rock and evergreen trees. To incorporate a Japanese flair, a near black brick with an evergreen tile roof was selected for the color scheme with natural log poles as accents.

ARCHITECT: JON R. SAYLER — SPOKANE VALLEY, WA.
BUILDER: SHAWN L GABLE — CHATTAROY, WA
DESIGNER: MARA NEWLUN — SPOKANE VALLEY, WA

*W*orking with the owners, interior designer Mara Newlun has achieved an exotic blend of two cultures. Using marble, limestone, granite, porcelain and hand painted tiles, the interior reflects the personality and lifestyle of the Higashi's. Animal accents in both the furniture and hardware have created what the Higshi's term their "Asian Safari." All interior woodwork on the cabinets, doors and trim is black walnut. The hand railing is steel and compliments the oriental flare of whimsical bamboo. The decor includes textured wall coverings and custom light fixtures.

Detailed straight lines are accentuated by the tile work and the vertical clear-grained ceilings found in the pool and entertainment rooms. The poolroom includes a de-humidifier and special wall construction to accommodate the humidity that comes with indoor pools and hot tubs.

The kitchen is a dream come true and features a 6 Dacor burner gas stove and custom range hood with a modern Asian flair. Dacor double ovens, black walnut cabinets and black granite backsplashes and countertops all add to the perfect ambiance for chefs of all expertise.

*B*oth outside patios, front driveway and walkways are heated for snowmelt. Guests are welcomed by a driveway that is embedded with a brick circle and the Japanese symbol for Higashi in the center.

155

The Knight Residence

FRIDAY HARBOR, WASHINGTON

Photography by Michael Mathers

David and Robin Knight have turned their hobby into a 27 year career they both love, building unique homes one house at a time. Each home has elements of previous ones, yet always incorporate new and different features. Their goal is to create homes that look like they came from another era, when talented artisans could spend the time necessary to make one-of-a-kind homes. Their homes begin with stone foundations that make the home appear to have sprouted from stone and to have been there forever. The rocks of the building flow into the gardens. The surrounding landscape is integrated with the house and defined by retaining walls, pools, and planting borders built of the same rock. The traditional home style includes steep, complicated rooflines. The overall effect is one of solidarity, strength, and security.

ARCHITECT, BUILDER & INTERIOR DESIGN:
DAVID AND ROBIN KNIGHT – FRIDAY HARBOR, WA

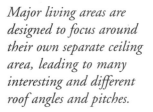

Major living areas are designed to focus around their own separate ceiling area, leading to many interesting and different roof angles and pitches.

Dormers and towers make the upstairs bedrooms charming and individually unique. Interior spaces influence the exterior look and are designed to also provide protected entryways and covered deck areas for the home.

Instead of doorways, public rooms have generous openings where the contents of one spill into the next. With the main living spaces overlapping one another, the result is longer views and a sense of inclusion. Heavy timbers and stone give the areas substantial bearing that is also snug and cozy. The home also delights with decorative features involving leaded glass, shaped rafted ends and intricate stucco patterns. Every window in the home is made using stained and leaded glass windows.

Spread information source:
Fine Home Building, Summer 2002

Cozy on
Bainbridge
Island

BAINBRIDGE ISLAND, WA

Photography by Michael Mathers

This quaint beachfront cottage on the Sound has it all; style, comfort and majestic views. The owners worked closely with the architect and builder to create a cozy family retreat that is truly unique and comfortable. The architect, Peter Brachvogel AIA, refers to his creation as "a whimsical interpretation of a 1920's cottage by the sea". The home is complemented magnificently by the impressive landscaping with the perfect combination of plants and foliage to accentuate the home and its wonderful setting. One of the Northwest's premier landscape artists, Patrick Leuner, took great care to compliment the exterior grounds with the perfect combination of plants and foliage to accentuate the home and its wonderful setting.

ARCHITECT: BC&J ARCHITECTURE/PETER BRACHVOGEL, AIA, PRINCIPAL IN CHARGE – BAINBRIDGE ISLAND, WA
BUILDER: W.M. CORBIN CONSTRUCTION CORP. – BAINBRIDGE ISLAND, WA

A glass walled dining area that juts off by the kitchen and family room provides for casual dining while enjoying all that Puget Sound and the Seattle skyline have to offer.

Directly above the glass enclosed dining area is an open air, rounded balcony off the master bedroom. The balcony rewards individuals with an impressive view of the Sound, Mt. Baker, and Mt. Rainier. Lots of beachfront decking makes for further enjoyment of these intoxicating views.

The craftsmanship that has gone into the wood-working is nothing short of fabulous, right down to the lighthouse shaped stairway and banister posts. This nautical theme is used in many areas, utilizing a ship's ladder to reach a loft sleeping area, and to provide a Cape Cod type environment throughout the home. The guesthouse and garage continue the New England beach house ambiance.

The End of the
Rainbow

First trial runs , October 1949 on Lake Washington, reached 150-160 miles per hour.

The property was a marvel of its time, designed by internationally renowned architect, Roland Terry, the "father of Northwest architecture", who created unique, grand spaces with understated luxury.

HUNTS POINT, WASHINGTON

Photography by Michael Mathers

This stunning Hunt's Point waterfront property is the jewel of Lake Washington. This two acre level parcel of land encompasses the entire tip of Hunt's Point, has 846 linear feet of prime Lake Washington waterfront, and offers 270 degree views that include the Seattle skyline and surrounding mountains. This 6,860 square foot home was built in 1950 by the pioneer of Seattle hydroplane racing, Stan Sayers.

Stan Sayers is regarded as the individual responsible for bringing hydroplane racing superiority to Seattle. The city fathers invented *SEAFAIR* as a summer celebration focal point for the community, but lacked a headline event to draw the crowds until Sayers took his locally designed, record setting Slo-mo-shun IV hydroplane to Detroit and brought home the prestigious Gold Cup trophy to Seattle. Slo-mo-shun IV held onto the cup for five straight years, providing Seattle with the impetus to launch and establish the SeaFair as one of the nation's most outstanding summer events. The Slo-mo-shun IV racing team became a rallying point for the city, and with the boat being moored at Hunts Point, this property quickly became the place for post race celebrations and the center of the Seattle racing world.

ARCHITECT: ROLAND TERRY – SEATTLE, WA

B/W Photos: Opposite page and below by Mary Randlett

Stan Sayers and Anchor Jensen preparing for Slo-mo-shun IV first test run. (1949)

165

*T*he glass walled sunken living room was built with enough room for two grand pianos and provides light filled openness. The property includes many amenities; impressive marble fireplace, spacious manicured lawns, expansive gardens, very private pool area, historical boathouse and dock, and a swimming cove with a sandy beach. These are but a few examples that demonstrate why this exquisite home is regarded as one of the most notable sites in North America and has earned it the title of "The End of the Rainbow".

The home boasts great attention to style and detail with custom features like this fish-shaped swimming pool.

The Fanch Retreat
at Wing Point

BAINBRIDGE, WASHINGTON

Photography by Michael Mathers

Located at the very tip of Wing Point on Bainbridge Island, this home is the epitome of the home selection criteria, "location - location - location". With 330 degrees of captivating, world-class views, this location is second to none.

From the golden aura of sunrise over the cityscape of Seattle, to the twinkling of city night-lights and star-studded skies, the views are nothing less than breathtaking. A cozy bench on the point at the very tip of the land presents everything the Sound has to offer, as well as unparalleled views of both Mt. Baker and Mt. Rainier.

ARCHITECT & BUILDER: 1901 –
THE BLACK FAMILY

Everyone traveling to Bainbridge Island by ferry gets a bird's eye view of the property on the right side, as they are about to enter the port. The distinguished flagpole placed by Senator Magnuson at the extreme tip is usually the first sight many visitors to the island will see.

Remodeled by the Senator, the home now belongs to the Fanch family who furnished it to suit their warm and comfortable family oriented lifestyle.

The home is almost hidden from view by the towering trees and lush landscaping, providing a feeling of privacy and serenity with a window to the world.

Two-story window walls (pictures top and opposite) fill up space between the interconnected beams and provide wide-open views of Haro Straight. The interior furnishings blend with the natural colors of grays, golds and greens of the rocks and water plus the burgundy accents from the madrone trunks.

SAN JUAN ISLAND, WASHINGTON

Photography by Steven Young

The challenge of constructing a home without disturbing the environment, where eagles nest in the high altitudes and Orcas feed in the rich waters below, has been achieved with overwhelming success with this beautiful home. Before a hammer was lifted, critical planning was essential. The landscape of rocks and native vegetation created natural boundaries for this 7.5 acre property and the views called for thoughtful design. Emerging from the rocky hillside, the 3,700 square foot residence on Lime Kilm Point has not only become a part of the landscape, but has succeeded in blending and improving the natural habitat around it.

LANDSCAPE ARCHITECT: RANDY ALLWORTH – WASHINGTON

With an emphasis on minimal disturbance of the natural surroundings, the landscaping on the property compliments nature and provides the owners with scenic overlooks. Serviceberry, Oregon Grape, Pacific Wax Myrtle and Sedum blend perfectly with the existing vegetation.

Lime Kilm Point
Residence

*T*he wide-open space of the great room runs
continuously through both the kitchen and dining
areas (above and opposite top right). They are artisti-
cally separated by the sculptural copper flue and a five
feet change in grade. The wide-open kitchen features
maple cabinets and limestone countertops. Retractable
patio doors open to the rear patio, the outdoor grill
and greenhouse.

The master bedroom (opposite top left) extends the focus
on views while the double-sided fireplace provides
warmth for both the master bedroom and the bath.
Relaxing in the bathtub comes easy when glancing out
the bay window while enjoying the comfort of the fire.

The home presents a never-ending offering of outside art and entertainment. Even the office that features mahogany floors, bookcases and a desk with space for two, presents views that equal or surpass any big city high-rise.

Within easy reach of the U.S. mainland and with whales, eagles, dolphins and porpoises providing constant enjoyment, the residence at Lime Kiln Point has captured the best of both indoor living and outdoor exhilaration.

Rainbow Rock Residence

LOPEZ ISLAND
WASHINGTON

Photography by Steve Keating

From the shimmering vistas of Lopez Island in the stunning San Juan's, you will find this spectacular 5,272 square foot vacation home designed by the architectural firm of Balance Associates Architects of Seattle.

The Rainbow Rock Residence is an example of the firm's mission of resisting the limitations of a particular architectural genre. Instead, they integrate vision, lifestyle and site while designing structures that reflect the personality of the owners and blend seamlessly with the surroundings.

ARCHITECT & INTERIOR:
    BALANCE ASSOCIATES, ARCHITECTS — SEATTLE, WA
BUILDER: RAVENHILL CONSTRUCTION — FRIDAY HARBER, WA

"*Good design does not require the triumph of form over function, but balance between the two...*"

The site's natural beauty guided a design that blurs the distinction between indoor and outdoor space. The rocky high bank waterfront site is naturally terraced into two platforms separated by a twenty-foot rock face. The house is located on the lower terrace while the upper terrace was left undeveloped for an outdoor play field. Connecting these terraces is a stair tower and bridge spanning the cliff.

A flexible floor plan provides space for large groups of friends and family while still being intimate in scale for a private weekend getaway for two. The house is divided into three masses – guest wing, play wing, and main house with owner's suite above on a separate floor.

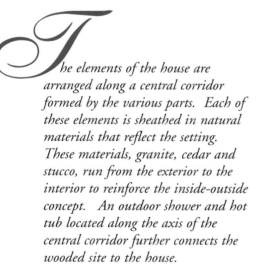

The elements of the house are arranged along a central corridor formed by the various parts. Each of these elements is sheathed in natural materials that reflect the setting. These materials, granite, cedar and stucco, run from the exterior to the interior to reinforce the inside-outside concept. An outdoor shower and hot tub located along the axis of the central corridor further connects the wooded site to the house.

A large outdoor terrace on the south side of the house is partially sheltered by a roof that becomes the cover for the living room. Enclosed by three sides of window walls, the living room has large sliding doors that connect it to the outdoor terrace. In contrast, solid forms of granite and wood give a sense of enclosure and shelter to the more private areas.

The home blends to perfection with the natural landscape as well as the genuine spirit of community and feeling for life found on Lopez Island.

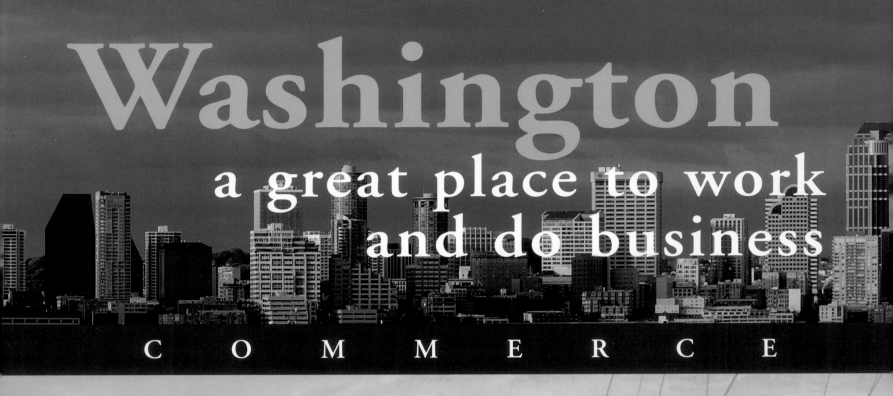

Washington
a great place to work and do business

COMMERCE

"The Evergreen State"

INDUSTRY

MAJOR INDUSTRIES OF WASHINGTON STATE

Architecture, Planning, Engineering

Aerospace

Agriculture - World Food Markets

Biotechnology

Education

Forestry

Health & Medical

Maritime

Outdoor Recreational Equipment

Software & Information Technology

Specialty Beverages

Telecommunications

Tourism

Washington's economy has continued to diversify over the past two decades resulting in a healthy climate for business investment as well as creating markets for a wide array of products and services. Known worldwide for its agricultural and forestry products, expansion into machinery, high technology electronics and the biotechnology industries has considerably broadened the economic base. Since no single industry dominates, fluctuations in specific sectors have less dramatic effects on the cumulative state economy.

Compared to figures nationally, Washington's labor force consistently ranks in the top five in terms of education, productivity and experience. The state's highly trained and skilled work force permits the economy to focus on industries of the future.

Washington is home to industry leaders in aerospace, computer software, biotechnology, telecommunications and other hi-tech sectors and is recognized for its innovative entrepreneurial culture. From e-commerce to gourmet coffee and customer service, worldwide trends have started or been cultivated in Washington.

ARCHITECTURE, PLANNING, ENGINEERING

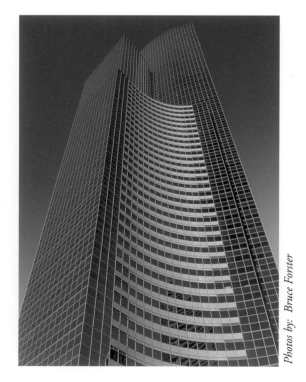

Photos by: Bruce Forster

Photos by: Martin Bylachek

The transformation of Seattle from a wilderness outpost to a city with one of the most recognized and coveted metropolitan landscapes is one where the poetry of design advocates the value to all human endeavor. The skyline is alive with buildings that are designed using nature's canvas as a background and the integration of man with environment is a model for future generations. Thanks in part to all of the people and firms -- past and present -- involved in the planning, engineering and design of one of the world's most livable cities.

With a growing population expanding into urban areas and a highly diversified economy, the State of Washington has constantly risen beyond the challenges of providing professional expertise and expression in architectural design, planning and engineering to meet and surpass the needs of the state in the 21st century. As a national center for manufacturing, high technology, trade and tourism, Seattle's reputation for highly specialized architecture, urban design and regional planning is met by a number of firms known worldwide for their highly specialized knowledge and skills.

Washington firms have brought their skills to high rise buildings in several different countries, have designed major department stores and mixed-use shopping complexes throughout the world, and designed passenger terminal buildings that serve airports across the country. They have designed specialty hospitals for cancer treatment, children's medicine and women's health care, biomedical research facilities and long term care and assisted living centers in locales as diverse as Berlin, Seoul, Shanghai, Hanzou and Taiwan. Sophisticated educational facilities have been developed in Beijing, American Samoa and throughout the United States. They have participated in the design and engineering of convention centers in Brunei, Manila, Dallas, Denver and Baltimore and performing arts theaters in several major U.S. cities.

From shopping, convention, and performing arts centers, to high-rise structures and airport terminal buildings, Washington offers a special experience and expertise in architecture, landscape design and planning for both urban and natural spaces. With over 400 environmental services companies, Washington has one of the most significant concentrations of environmental planning and engineering firms in the world. The success of the states architectural designers and planners is seen not only by the integration of man with the environment, but by the many companies who choose to locate their headquarters here as a result of an international reputation for both business quality and way of life.

Photos by: Martin Bylachek

AEROSPACE

Washington was an important center of the defense industry during World War II, partly because of the immense aircraft industry in Seattle. Today, the aerospace industry continues to be a significant component of the manufacturing economy of the state. At present, roughly one out of every four manufacturing jobs is directly engaged in the aerospace industry.

Washington State is home to the Boeing Commercial Airplane Company. With 60 percent of the world's commercial air fleet, Boeing is the leading manufacturer of large commercial aircraft in the global aerospace arena. Boeing aircraft exports represent more than a quarter of the state's total exports. The company's decision to offer the new 7E7 Dreamliner to the market will create some of the most momentous changes to the local aerospace market in a decade.

Aerospace in Washington, however, is more that The Boeing Company. Washington is also home to over 300 aerospace companies and hundreds of suppliers and service firms. These companies manufacture a wide variety of parts and supplies and market to aerospace companies throughout the world.

Photos by: Bruce Forster

AGRICULTURE -
WORLD FOOD MARKETS

Washington State is one of the largest and most diversified exporters of food and agriculture products in the United States. Known worldwide for quality, variety and year-round availability, it maintains a solid reputation as an agricultural powerhouse.

The state's rich, arable lands are nurtured by a mild climate and a growing season filled with warm days and cool nights. The geography and unique landscapes have allowed the state to diversify with a myriad of agriculture products. The Cascade Mountain Range creates micro-climates that support record crop diversity while a full third of the state is in pastureland or rangeland supporting the cattle industry. The bounty from the Pacific Ocean supports a thriving seafood industry and it's not surprising that hops are a top crop that support Washington's ever-growing micro-brew beer

Photos by: Larry Conboy

production. Located at approximately the same latitude as the great wine regions of France, with long warm days and cool crisp nights, the state is recognized world-wide for its premium wines.

Washington enjoys a distinct natural geographic advantage and is a crossroad to the world. Western Washington ports are the closest Continental U.S. ports to Northern Asia. The ports of Seattle and Tacoma are the second-largest container hubs in the United States and the Seattle-Tacoma International Airport is equidistant to both Tokyo and London, supporting exports of perishable items.

Today, the agri-food complex employs more than any other sector in the state. With its natural wealth, proximity to world markets, world-class transportation and port facilities, state of the art food processing and cutting-edge research and technology, Washington continues to be a leader in the field of food exports and agricultural products.

Photos by: Charles Gurche

BIOTECHNOLOGY

Photos by: Bruce Forster

The Seattle metropolitan area and Washington State is now recognized as one of the premier biotechnology and medical technology centers in the world and one of the fastest growing research centers in the United States. This is an industry that is founded on the state's world-class research institutions, entrepreneurial spirit, rapidly growing financial wealth, and unsurpassed quality of life that makes it one of the most desirable places to work, live and play.

Biotechnology and medical technology companies in Washington are developing revolutionary methods for the diagnosis and treatment of cancer, AIDS, cystic fibrosis, multiple sclerosis, rheumatoid arthritis and other serious conditions.

The technology foundation of Washington's industry is the cutting edge research conducted at the University of Washington, Washington State University, the Fred Hutchinson Cancer Research Center, and Pacific Northwest National Laboratory. In fact, more than one-half of the more than 170 biotechnology and medical device firms in the state are founded on technologies developed at these institutions.

As we enter the 21st century, we are witnessing the convergence of biotechnology and medical technology. This convergence, combined with the state's existing strengths in electrical engineering, software development, and semiconductor design and fabrication will position Washington State at the forefront of new technology research development well into the next century, nationally, as well as globally.

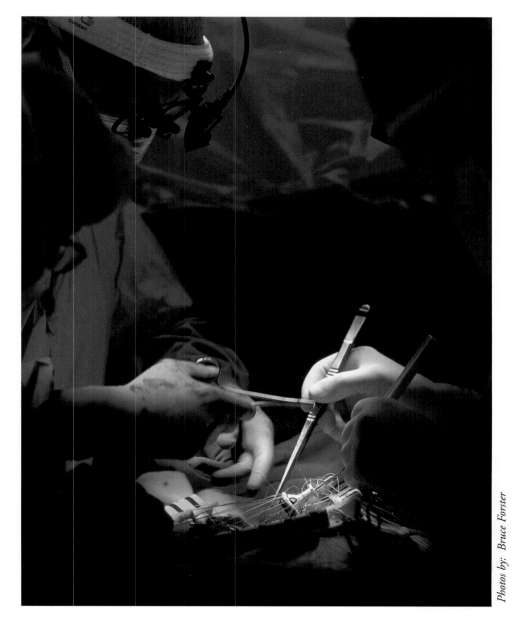

Photos by: Bruce Forster

FORESTRY

Photos by: Steve Terrill

Washington State is home to approximately 21 million acres of forestland. Over 48 percent of the land in Washington is forested, a much higher ratio than the national average of 33 percent. Forty-four percent of the forestland is owned by public agencies, 20 percent by private industry and 19 percent by non-industrial private owners.

Because of its abundant forest resources, its location on the Pacific coast, and its geographical features suitable for port facilities, Washington State is the largest exporter of forest products in the United States. Of all US forest products exports, 12.2 percent leave from ports in Washington.

Washington's forest management focuses on ecologically sustainable production, assuring a continuous resource supply with minimal reduction in biological diversity. Washington's commitment to protecting its forest-lands has resulted in some of the nation's most comprehensive and innovative forest practices rules.

Photos by: Bruce Forster

HEALTH & MEDICAL

Greater Seattle is recognized around the world as a center for exciting and ground-breaking medical research. Researchers at educational institutions, independent facilities, and biomedical and biotechnology companies have earned the reputation for innovative basic science and clinical investigations. Formal research partnerships allow Greater Seattle researchers to work with colleagues in other countries to improve the health of people worldwide.

Photos by: Martin Bylachek

The Fred Hutchinson Cancer Research Center houses the largest program in the world devoted to cancer prevention and control research. The Department of Molecular Biotechnology was established at the University of Washington in 1992 with a $12 million gift from Microsoft chairman Bill Gates. Seattle Biomedical Research Institute, in partnership with German researchers, is investigating the parasite that causes "sleeping sickness" in Africa. The UW operates the world's largest clinical training program for sexually transmitted diseases, including HIV/AIDS.

The Greater Seattle region is home to more than a half dozen major hospitals and medical centers that provide health care for patients from across the nation and other countries.

Photos by: Bruce Forster

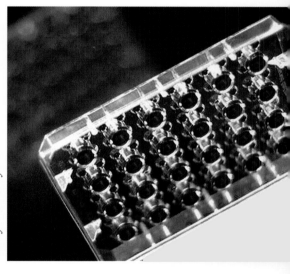

Photos by: Martin Bylachek

These institutions are equipped with the latest in medical technology and are staffed by highly-skilled medical professionals, many of whom are internationally respected. The hospitals consistently rank among the most efficient in the nation on all measures of hospital use.

EDUCATION

UNIVERSITY OF WASHINGTON

Washington State possess one of the finest public and private university and college systems in the United States. Washington is home to more than 21 four-year state and independent universities and colleges. The states major research universities, the University of Washington and Washington State University, have been nationally recognized for their ground breaking work in many of today's top fields, making them a premier destination for international scholars.

Founded in 1861, the University of Washington (UW) is one of the oldest state-supported institutions of higher education on the Pacific coast. The University is comprised of three campuses: the Seattle campus is made up of seventeen schools and colleges whose faculty offer educational opportunities to students ranging from first-year undergraduates through doctoral-level candidates; the Bothell and Tacoma campuses, each developing a distinctive identity and undergoing rapid growth, offer diverse programs to upper-division undergraduates and to graduate students.

Ranked 1st overall in the state for its undergraduate programs, the University of Washington offers degrees in a multitude of areas. The computer science and engineering programs rank among the top 10 in the nation. The UW undergraduate business program is ranked 16th and its subsidiary international business program ranks 9th. The UW is currently host to over 2,400 international students who take advantage of its diverse program offerings.

The U.S. News and World Report rankings of best graduate schools listed 13 of the University of Washington's graduate programs in the top 25 in the nation, including the medicine, dentistry, nursing, public health and computer science programs.

The University of Washington has garnered attention for its landmark work in software development, cancer treatment, and integrated circuit design, among others. In early 1996, the UW was awarded a landmark grant of $12 million to set up a new engineering research center for the development of a completely new form of medical implants. In fact, the UW has been ranked first among public universities in the total amount of federal grants and contracts it received for research. As one of the nation's outstanding teaching and research institutions, the University is committed to maintaining an environment for objectivity and imaginative inquiry.

WASHINGTON STATE UNIVERSITY

Founded in Pullman in 1890, Washington State University (WSU) is the state's land-grant research university. It has campuses in Spokane, the Tri-Cities (Richland, Pasco and Kennewick) and Vancouver.

Located on College Hill, WSU's 620 acre campus is one of the largest residential campuses west of the Mississippi with about half of the student body living in residence halls, single and family student apartments and fraternity and sorority houses.

Washington State University offers a wide selection of outstanding academic programs, including several ranked among the best in the nation. WSU is known for research strengths in areas as diverse as biotechnology, shock physics, viticulture, sleep, wood technology, computer chips and advertising's impact on healthy decision-making.

The College of Engineering and Architecture offers an array of engineering programs including study in the areas of biological systems, chemical, civil, computer, electrical, manufacturing, materials, and mechanical engineering. The college is open to international students and offers practical applications in all engineering fields.

WSU maintains the largest agricultural education, outreach and research programs of the state's public and private institutions and corporations. The college has a long history of supporting research for the state's agriculture commissions and is nationally acclaimed for its plant biochemistry research and training facilities. WSU has recently received national recognition for research in biogenetics, high-yield and disease-resistant wheat strains and monoclonal antibodies.

MARITIME

Washington is an important center for both the commercial and the leisure marine sectors. The maritime industries here are diverse and mature, with everything from a major US Navy Trident nuclear submarine base to world-class kayak manufactures. Design firms, services and value added businesses are at the forefront of this important industry.

The ports of Greater Seattle provide one of the most efficient and economical gateways to the world. Together, the Ports of Seattle and Tacoma are the second-largest volume container center in the United States. These ports serve not only the Pacific Northwest, but also the major cities of the Midwest, East Coast and Canada. Seattle is one sailing day closer to Asia than the California ports, offering time and cost savings to importers and exporters alike.

One quarter of the jobs in Washington State are related to trade and the maritime and fisheries industries. In fact, Washington is the most trade-dependent state in the nation and the Puget Sound is the most export dependent metropolitan area in the United States. Seattle is the homeport to the U.S. North Pacific fishing fleet and is the point of entry for 50 percent of the seafood caught in the United States. Salmon, pollock, cod, halibut and crab are among the principle seafood species caught in the healthy and abundant waters of the North Pacific. The commercial fishing sector provides for approximately 10,000 jobs and accounts for gross annual sales of more than $3.5 billion.

Greater Seattle is an important center for ship repair. There are eight major shipyards and over 20 smaller yards in the Greater Seattle area. The facilities concentrate on ship repair and the construction of ferries, tugboats, recreational and tourist vessels. Fresh water in-ways connecting to the saltwater sound provide an advantage for the shipyards and repair facilities. The fresh water kills saltwater marine growth on boat hulls and allows vessels to be worked on without the inconvenience of tidal action.

The waters of Greater Seattle make it a boaters' paradise. With one boat registered to one out of every five people, the area boasts the highest per-capita concentration of boaters in the United States. A number of firms are leaders in the design and engineering of marine vessels. From pleasure boats to naval ships to fishing vessels, these companies conduct work for clients all over the world.

OUTDOOR RECREATIONAL EQUIPMENT

Photos by: Martin Bylachek

The natural beauty and outdoor recreational opportunities found in Washington State are unsurpassed by few places anywhere. The diverse geography and distinct weather patterns in the state create one of the most unique regions in the world. In a state that has two mountain ranges, a rainforest, a desert, lakes, rivers and the Pacific Ocean, anyone who loves the outdoors is certain to find an activity to match their interests. And the manufactures of outdoor recreational equipment have followed suit by creating an industry here that meets and surpasses the needs of almost every out-door enthusiast.

Encouraged by Greater Seattle's high-tech environment, local companies have evolved into world-class manufacturers of recreational equipment by creating new and innovative products. Washington State is home to over 35 manufacturers of outdoor recreational equipment, generating a variety of products, including but not limited to, an assortment of camping and climbing gear products, mountain biking equipment, recreational boating, fishing equipment, and, of course, snow gear. The outdoor apparel and sportswear attire found here are state of the art and specifically designed for extreme weather and other outdoor conditions. Washington's manufacturers supply the equipment and meet the demands.

The three national parks within easy driving distance of the metro area, the technological capabilities spun out of the many industrial giants in Seattle, and the rampant entrepreneurial endeavors of the citizens certainly contributed to the formation of Seattle's outdoor equipment industry. However, the critical ingredient was a large and well-trained population ready to take to the great oudoors.

Photos by: Martin Bylachek

Photos by: Martin Bylachek

Washington State is gifted with skiing unsurpassed in accessibility and variety of terrain. Venture two hours or less from any metropolitan area in the state and the views of snow-capped peaks and volcanoes are so breathtaking, no photograph could ever do them justice. Washington is blessed with an amazing array of salt and fresh water recreation areas where boaters head to the mountain lakes or Puget Sound while windsurfers head to the Gorge. River possibilities for kayakers are endless and include sea kayaking in the Olympic Peninsula.

Washington is like heaven for hikers. No matter where you are in the state, you're never far from a trail. Or feel like fishing? Grab yourself a rod, reel and cast away for some of the finest fishing in the country. No matter what your outdoor pleasure, you will find in Washington. Chances are, the equipment being used to enhance the experience will be manufactured "in house".

SOFTWARE & INFORMATION TECHNOLOGY

Washington States economy is a solid mixture of diversity and the software and information technology businesses are contributing more than ever. Almost daily, technology is transforming business at every level; internally, locally, nationally, and globally, and Seattle is among the world leaders in providing established and innovative services.

Seattle's high tech sector includes software and internet-based companies as well as advanced technology manufacturers. Companies are drawn to the area for its educated workforce, the vital downtown area that is a great place to live, work and play, and the universities and learning centers with their world-class research and educational opportunities. The number of prominent and dynamic hi-tech and biotech firms already located here is another major appeal for bringing new businesses to the area.

Photos by: Bruce Forster

The Information Technology field is growing two times faster than any other segment of the economy. A recent Department of Labor study indicates that more than a million new IT jobs will be created in the United States by the year 2005, and Washington is one of the world's leading centers for software development and information technology. It is home to over 3,000 software companies, including Microsoft, the world's largest software company; Nintendo of America, the video game powerhouse; and Attachmate, one of the largest privately-held software companies in the world. Washington State information technology companies are trend-setters which have created a culture of innovation.

The industry generates more than $25 billion in revenue each year and has become one of the state's most important. Employment in the software and computer-related sector of Washington State is 15 percent higher than the national average. Greater Seattle ranks fifth among U.S. metropolitan areas for number of software jobs as percentage of the total population, according to a recent study. Nearly 70,000 people are employed in the industry totaling $10 billion in wages.

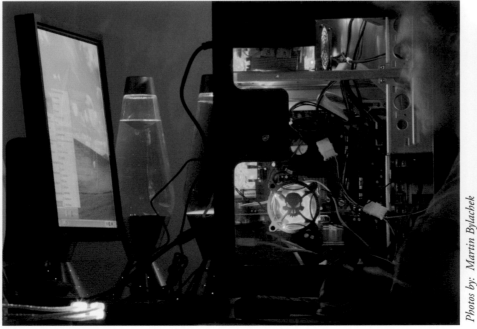

Photos by: Martin Bylachek

Photos by: Martin Bylachek

SPECIALTY BEVERAGES

Photos by: Bruce Forster

*W*ashington's specialty beverage industry has an option for every thirst. Three of the world's largest coffeehouse brands are here and Washington is the second largest producer and exporter of wines in the United States. In addition to coffee and wine, Washington State is also a leading grower of hops, the basic ingredient used in brewing beer for the country's growing micro-brewing industry. In fact, Washington State is the leading grower of hops, accounting for 20 percent of the world output.

Famous for quality apples and an abundance of water, you can find pure bottled apple juice and natural spring water unsurpassed anywhere, and with coffeehouse brands like Starbucks, Seattle's Best Coffee and Tully's, Washington State is considered the epicenter of the "caffeine craze." Walk outside a building in downtown Seattle and the first thing you will see is someone holding a cup of coffee.

Washington State is the second largest producer and exporter of wines in the United States, an industry that generates more than $2.4 billion annually. Wine Enthusiast magazine named Washington State "wine region of the year" in 2001, an honor that takes into consideration all wine growing regions in the world.

Photos by: Bruce Forster

TELECOMMUNICATIONS

*T*elecommunications represents one of the emerging sectors of employment growth in Washington. Most of the growth in the state has occurred in the Greater Seattle area and came from newer telecommunications services such as cellular, paging, satellite services, data and video transmission.

Washington State is one of the world's leading centers for software development with over 1,600 companies statewide. The original McCaw Cellular - now AT&T Wireless Services - was founded here and became the seed that produced a cluster of related advanced telecommunications companies. McCaw Cellular did for wireless communications what Microsoft did for software and Boeing did for aerospace.

Washington companies in the telecommunications industry have discovered niches in manufacturing, installing and servicing the basic infrastructure. As a manufacturing center, these companies make the equipment that is the core technological components for telecommunications.

In 1996, the Washington State legislature recognized the critical role of technology in education and authorized the building of the $55 million K-20 Educational Telecommunications Network. Believed to be the first of its kind in the nation, the K-20 Network resulted in a high-speed telecommunications network that enables the use of the Internet and live two-way video conferencing in all of Washington's public educational sectors. The K-20 Network helps educators stretch limited resources and students gain skills for jobs in a competitive marketplace.

Photos by: Bruce Forster

Photos by: Bruce Forster

TOURISM

Washington State's diverse culture, along with an extremely varied geography and climate, has created one of the America's richest traveling experiences. Washington offers the tourist all the amenities of a major metropolitan city, some of the country's best recreational and scenic rivers, the Pacific Ocean, magnificent snow capped mountains, a rich and diverse agricultural region, the desert, a rainforest, islands, gorges, glaciers, and an abundance of wildlife from eagles to Orca whales. In short, when you toss in more natural wonders than can be explored in a lifetime, you have the Washington tourist experience.

The states $11 billion travel and tourism industry provides more than 127,000 jobs and consists primarily of small businesses. Although about one-half of all travel jobs are located in the Seattle metropolitan area, the counties that have the highest number of travel-generated jobs in relation to total employment are in rural areas, and this helps to make travel-generated employment in the rural areas a substantial part of their economy.

Photos by: Martin Bylachek

Part of the reason for the successful tourist trade in rural areas is that the outdoor scenic and recreational opportunities throughout the state are so accessible it's almost too easy. Road trips are common and there are almost as many miles of roads as there are scenic attractions. The Cascade Loop is a well-traveled area that traverses inland taking visitors through many small mountain towns and scenic attractions. Since Washington is also the smallest state west of the Rockies, the visitor can easily travel the varied parts of this gifted corner of the continental U.S.

Each of the state's regions offers a unique charm and wide array of activities. Seattle and the Puget Sound are loaded with shopping, fine dining, sightseeing, boating, and a full range of professional sports teams. The Cascade Mountains are a short drive east of the coast and include such landmarks as Mount St. Helens, Mount Rainier and the Snoqualmie Pass. The Cascades also offer unlimited resources for outdoor sports including hiking, biking, camping, and skiing. In the central part of the state lies the rich agricultural country with an abundance of farms and orchards. Further east, the Columbia River Basin presents many wonders including the Grand Coulee Dam, which is the largest concrete dam in North America and the third largest producer of electricity worldwide. Spokane is the largest city in eastern Washington and offers an abundance of scenic and outdoor recreational adventures. From natural wonders like rainforests, towering volcanoes, and the Columbia Gorge, to manmade structures like the Space Needle and the Grand Coulee Dam, it's no wonder that tourists from the far corners of the world choose to experience Washington.

The Washington State Tourism Office works to strengthen the state's economy through the promotion of Washington as a year-round travel destination. The office implements domestic and international marketing and tourism development programs with an emphasis on increasing off-season travel to the rural and under-visited areas of the state.

Photos by: Holland America Line, MS Veendam, Seattle

Craftsmen
& Designer Credits

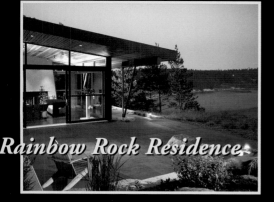

Rainbow Rock Residence

ARCHITECTS & INTERIORS:
Balance Associates, Architects
(206) 322-7737
101 Euclid Avenue
Seattle, WA 98122
www.balanceassociates.com

GENERAL CONTRACTOR:
Ravenhill Construction
PO Box 888
Friday Harbor, WA 98250
(360) 378-5404

ARCHITECT: Jon R. Sayler, AIA. PS.
204 S. Koren Rd. Ste 700
Spokane Valley, WA 99212
(509) 535-9207   saylerjr@qwest.net
INTERIOR DESIGNER: Debbie Shaffer
DGS Interiors, 223 N. Bellevue Avenue
Walla Walla, WA 99362
(509) 522-9419

Double River Ranch

Lady Lola Yacht

BUILDER:
Oceanco/2002
Guildo Pastor Centre
7 Rue de Gabian
MC9800, Monaco
+37 7 93 10 02 80
INTERIOR DESIGNER:
Franco Zuretti
Zuretti Interior Designers

ARCHITECT & BUILDER: Tom Kelly
Neil Kelly Designers/Remodeler
804 N. Alberta
Portland, OR 97217
(503) 288-7461
www.neilkelly.com

Snyder's Snug Harbor

Publisher:
RhinoBooks
www.rhinobooks.net

The House at Eagle Bluff

ARCHITECT: Jon R. Sayler, AIA. PS.
204 S. Koren Rd. Ste 700
Spokane Valley, WA 99212
(509) 535-9207   saylerjr@qwest.net
BUILDER: Dan Olson
Daniel J. Olson Construction, Inc.
P.O. Box 13246
Spokane, WA 99213
(509) 928-9209   dan@gntech.net
INTERIOR DESIGNER: Mara Newlun
R. Alan Brown, Inc.
E. 10303 Sprague
Spokane Valley, WA 99206
(509) 939-9381

BUILDER: Terry Thompson
Thompson Residential Development
2812 120th Avenue NE
Bellevue, WA 98005
(425) 466-8491   terrya2@mindspring.com
INTERIOR DESIGNER: Sally Thompson
Sally's Interior Design
Bellevue, WA 98005
(425) 702-9215 terrya2@mindspring.com

Livable Art at Pike's Peak

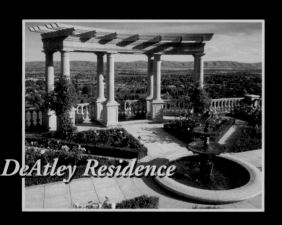

DeAtley Residence

ARCHITECT & INTERIOR ARCHITECTURE:
Vassos M. Demetriou
Demetriou Architects
5555 Lakeview Dr., Suite 200
Kirkland, WA 98003
(425) 827-1700   VMD@demetriou.net
www.demetriouarchitects.com
INTERIOR DESIGNER:
Edward Maske & Joe Simon
Shopkeeper
3105 Summitview Avenue
Yakima, WA 98902
(509) 452-6646 or (888) 577-2356
shopkpr@aol.com - www.shopkpr.com

ARCHITECT: Norman Sandler
Sandler Kilburn Architects, LLC
1661 E. Olive Way, Suite 200
Seattle, WA 98102
(206) 682-5211
www.sandlerarchitects.com
BUILDER: Denny Howell
Shawnee Construction, LLC
2613 Meadow Avenue N
Renton, WA 98056   (425) 226-5160
denny@shawneeconstructionllc.com
www.shawneeconstructionllc.com
INTERIOR DESIGNER: Elisabeth Beers
Sandler Kilburn Architects, LLC
1661 E. Olive Way, Suite 200
Seattle, WA 98102

First Hill Living in Seattle

In Harmony With Puget Sound

BUILDER: Donna Shirey CGR, CAPS
Shirey Contracting Incorporation
230 NE Juniper Street
Issaquah, WA 98027
(425) 427-1300
donna@shireycontracting.com
www.shireycontracting.com

ARCHITECT:
Robert Deson Swair
5339 Ballard Ave. N.W.
Seattle, WA 98107
(206) 784-4822
INTERIOR DESIGNER:
Doug Rasar Interior Design
9400 Vineyard Crest
Bellevue, WA 98004
(425) 450-9911
Rasarinterior@qwest.net

North Bend Estate

Cozy on Bainbridge Island

ARCHITECT & INTERIOR DESIGNERS:
Peter Brachvogel, AIA
BC&J Architects PS
197 Parfitt Way SW, Suite 120
Bainbridge Isl, WA 98110
(206) 780-9113
peterb@bcandj.com   www.bcandj.com
BUILDER:
Bill Corbin
W.M. Corbin Const. Corp.
8719 Battle Point Rd. NE
Bainbridge Isl, WA 98110
(206) 842-5538   buildcorbin@yahoo.com

ARCHITECT:
Jon R. Sayler AIA, P.S.
204 S. Koren Rd., Suite 700
Spokane Valley, WA
(509) 535-9207
saylerjr@qwest.net

BUILDER:
Gable Woodworking & Constrution
N. 26715 Ptarmigan Dr.
Chattaroy, WA 99003
(509) 238-4427

INTERIOR DESIGNER:
Mara Newlun
R. Alan Brown, Inc.
East 10303 Sprague
Spokane Valley, WA 99206
(509) 939-9381

The Higashi Residence

Publisher:
RhinoBooks, LLC
www.rhinobooks.net